Praise for *Deliver the Unexpected*

"Richard's insights are exactly what entrepreneurs need to read to transform their business in today's new reality."

—Margaret Kelly, CEO of RE/MAX International

"Much more than just a fascinating story and much more than just a book on success. Be ready to come away with a knowledge of the principles that will help you take your career and income to a whole new level."

—Bob Burg, Co-author of *The Go-Giver*
and author of *Endless Referrals*

"This is a terrific book—entertaining, insightful, and fast-moving. You learn a series of proven, practical methods and techniques to help you build and run a more profitable business."

—Brian Tracy, Chairman & CEO,
Brian Tracy International

"Anyone can beat up on common wisdom. The trick is building something better in its place and Robbins has done it—big time. Highly recommended."

—Michael Port, Author of *The Contrarian Effect:
Why It Pays (BIG) to Take Typical Sales Advice
and Do The Opposite*

"*Deliver the Unexpected* is an absolute must-read for any entrepreneur serious about changing the game."

—Robin Sharma, Author of the #1 bestsellers
The Leader Who Had No Title and *The Monk Who Sold His Ferrari*

DELIVER
THE
UNEXPECTED

DELIVER THE UNEXPECTED

And 6 Other New Truths for Business Success

RICHARD ROBBINS

WILEY

John Wiley & Sons, Inc.

Cover design: Michael J. Freeland

Published by John Wiley & Sons, Inc., Hoboken, New Jersey.
Published simultaneously in Canada.

For general information on our other products and services or for technical support,
please contact our Customer Care Department within the United States at (800) 762-2974,
outside the United States at (317) 572-3993 or fax (317) 572-4002.

Wiley publishes in a variety of print and electronic formats and by print-on-demand.
Some material included with standard print versions of this book may not be included in
e-books or in print-on-demand. If this book refers to media such as a CD or DVD that is
not included in the version you purchased, you may download this material at http://
booksupport.wiley.com. For more information about Wiley products, visit
www.wiley.com.

ISBN 978-1-118-40231-3 (cloth); ISBN 978-1-118-46159-4 (ebk);
ISBN 978-1-118-46161-7 (ebk); ISBN 978-1-118-46163-1(ebk)

Printed in the United States of America.

10 9 8 7 6 5 4 3 2 1

This book is dedicated to my parents,
Larry and Margaret Robbins,
who have always believed in me far
more than I ever could.

Contents

Acknowledgments   xi

Introduction   1

1 The Sign   5

2 The Nemesis   15

3 The Cub   29

4 The Future Myth   45

5 The Knowledge Myth   71

6 The Failure Myth   95

7 The Abundance Myth   115

8 The Value Myth   137

9 The Attraction Myth   155

10 The Journal   183

11 The Shop   189

12 The Happiness Myth   197

Acknowledgments

All great projects (and you, the reader, will decide whether this is a great project) are the result of not one person, but rather a team of inspired individuals who come together for a common cause. It is with my greatest admiration and appreciation that I acknowledge the following people—without each and every one of them, this dream would not be a reality.

First and foremost, my wife, Sue Robbins, the smartest, most compassionate, kind, caring, and selfless person I have ever known. I still wonder every day how I got so lucky. Sue is as much a part of this project as I am.

My kids, Jaimie and Tanner, who are my greatest inspiration. Every day I do my best work in hopes of making them proud.

My parents, to whom this book is dedicated, who for as long as I can remember, in my darkest days, have said it is always going to be okay, and in my brightest moments are my biggest cheerleaders.

Acknowledgments

Dan Clements, my writer, who took the time to attend my seminars, watch my videos, read my writings, and spend countless hours with me on the phone to capture my voice in print. Dan is a gifted writer and my only hope is that this is not the end of our partnership, but just the beginning.

The entire RRi team, our cherished extended family. It humbles me to watch how much they believe in what we do as an organization and the lengths they will go to *Deliver the Unexpected* to the people we have the privilege of serving.

Our editors at Wiley, who patiently guided us through the complicated process of publishing a book and held us accountable to the deadlines required to see this project to the finish.

Resources to Help You *Deliver the Unexpected*

The end of this book marks the beginning of what could be the greatest journey you have ever experienced in your business. Visit www.richardrobbins .com and learn what to do next! Find free resources, downloads, and implementation ideas to help you deliver the unexpected.

Acknowledgments

Richard Robbins International Inc. is a results-focused training organization dedicated to empowering sales and business professionals to build businesses that fully support the lives they want to live. Visit www.richard robbins.com for information on booking Richard to speak, upcoming live events, free resources, video blogs, and a wide range of sales and business coaching programs and services.

Follow Richard on Twitter:
www.twitter.com/RichardLRobbins

Connect with Richard personally on Facebook:
www.facebook.com/OfficialRichardRobbins

Introduction

When I began my career in sales, I was taught the most conventional sales strategy of all: *Outwork everyone else.*

For five years, I did just that. I was ambitious, and I sold harder, worked harder, and tried harder than my competition. I outran everyone.

Was I financially successful? Certainly. But over those years, a thought was beginning to percolate in the back of my mind: *No matter how many people you outrun, you're still running.*

Despite my success, I began to wonder if I was doing things wrong. Or perhaps even worse, I was doing the things right, but for the wrong *reasons.* I was successful, but was I professionally satisfied? Far from it—I yearned for a bigger challenge. Confident? Hardly—I was insecure, constantly trying to prove myself. Happier each year? Not a chance. I had no choice but to run harder each year as the treadmill sped up.

It was a thought that began to haunt me. And over time I began to realize I wasn't alone. *Lots* of people were running. Hard, fast, and long. What struck me, though, was that not all of them were *succeeding*. I was in the minority. Of all the entrepreneurs and salespeople out there, very few were reaching their potential. The markets for most industries were controlled by a few key businesses. The majority of sales were made by a handful of high performers. I began to realize that what most people were doing—even the ones running hard—just wasn't *working*.

For all that running, the vast majority of the world was stuck in mediocrity.

That breakthrough sent me on a new personal quest to understand success, and happiness. To discover why so many people settled for so much less than they were capable of. To define why success seemed so elusive for so many, despite their best efforts.

Four years later, I sold my business and began to teach what I'd learned. Today, that teaching continues. We help thousands of entrepreneurs and salespeople each year do the right things for the right reasons, and rise to their true potential.

This book—and the story of Josh—is, in many ways, my story. But I suspect it's also yours, and that of anyone else who has struggled with finding their way in business and life.

My hope is that all of our stories, like this one, have happy endings.

Richard Robbins

Chapter 1

The Sign

When Josh Abrams left the hotel that evening he had one thing on his mind: *success*. After the hugs, handshakes, and goodbyes, he had crossed the parking lot to his car like he was floating on air, the enthusiasm bubbling up through him.

Things were going to be okay.

No—better than okay. They were going to be *great*.

As he hit the freeway, he cranked up the radio and pounded on the steering wheel like a drummer about to spontaneously combust, punctuating the music with the occasional, "Woo!" and throwing his fist through the sunroof. He was pumped up. *Seriously* pumped up.

But, now, just hours later, as he sat dumbstruck in his car, he couldn't help but wonder: *How had things gone bad so quickly?*

■　■　■

The trouble began with the long trip home. Josh had driven nearly eight hours to get to the seminar. He'd thought of flying, of course, but there was no way Kiera was going to go for that. And she was right, if he stopped to think about it—it really *was* too expensive. And so in the end, he drove. But that was okay, because this weekend had really changed things. Next year at this time, he'd definitely be flying. Maybe first class. No, *definitely* first class.

For the first hour of the trip home, that was exactly how things seemed. As he drove west into a mind-blowing sunset, his mind racing a million miles an hour, he felt optimism on a whole new level. He even found himself pulling over to jot notes in the journal he'd received at the seminar. He knew he'd be even later getting home as a result. *But hey*, he told himself, *genius works on its own timeline, right?* Besides, he was finally going to be free. Going to straighten out his finances. Get his life in order. It was all coming together.

And then the sun went down.

The last of the sunset snuffed out with a final pink gasp, and then it was twilight. As if on cue, the radio, which had been pumping what seemed like "Josh Abrams' Greatest Hits Ever," turned to—well, Josh didn't know what it turned to, but it was as if he was suddenly driving a hearse instead of his leased Lexus. It was like someone had thrown a switch. The sun went down, and Josh's optimism sank with it. And not long after, the voice started. It was that same little voice in his head that always seemed to chime in at times like these.

This isn't the first time this has happened, the voice said.

Yeah, but this time's different, Josh thought.

Whatever.

He really *had* thought this was different. He'd been to other seminars—plenty of them, if he chose to admit it—but this guy was *really* good, the best of the best. He'd coached everyone from Silicon Valley startups to the sales elite across almost every industry. When Josh had first heard that his sales seminar was going to take place just a few hours away, it was like someone had thrown a drowning man a rope. But now, as the high of the weekend faded with the sun, Josh could feel the rope slipping through his fingers.

He'd set some fantastic goals this weekend. Sure, he'd declined the post-seminar coaching program—they were always trying to sell you that stuff—but the goals! He thought they would really change things for him and Kiera, but as darkness settled in, the doubt arrived with it.

Sure. Big goals, the voice said. *But now what?*

It was true. He'd been caught up in the buzz of the weekend and hadn't really thought about *how* he was going to make things happen when he went back to work—selling real estate—on Monday.

See?

Josh banished the voice from his mind. He flipped the radio to a new station—not quite as good as the first, but it would do—and concentrated on what he'd learned over the weekend. He looked over at his success journal on the seat, and began to—

—a horn blared loudly, and Josh jerked the wheel to the right. He'd nearly drifted into the other lane.

See, the voice said, *you're dreaming. You need to face reality.*

Josh closed the journal, and focused on the road ahead. It was going to be a long drive home.

As he drew closer to his house, though, his spirits began to rise again. "Just a little post-adrenaline crash," he said aloud.

The nearer to home he got, the more new ideas started to appear in his mind, and he jotted them down in his journal. This time, it was a different voice in his head that spoke up.

This could really work. Things are going to be fine.

The new voice might not sound as confident as he should, but that was okay, Josh figured, because, truth be told, he had a serious hole to climb out of.

He shifted in his seat as he turned onto their street. It was a fantastic neighborhood, but buying into it had been the start of the hole-digging that he and Kiera had been doing since they got married.

The house was a little more than they could comfortably afford. And it came on the heels of their wedding, which, though also fantastic, was a little extravagant. They were still paying for it. As well as the two new cars, the most recent of which was Josh's fully loaded luxury SUV that he told Kiera (and himself) was necessary for driving clients around. After gassing it up for the 16-plus hours of highway time this weekend, it had occurred to him more than once that perhaps he and his clients could get around in something a little smaller.

And, if he was truly honest, there weren't that many clients.

Their expanding lifestyle and deepening debt were the hole that he and Kiera were stuck in, but the current real estate market was burying them alive. The market had really started to slow after they'd bought their home, and Josh's real estate business had slowed right along with it. Even when he could find homes to sell, he had trouble moving the listings.

Kiera's job was stable—knock on wood—but their lifestyle most decidedly relied on two incomes. Josh needed to contribute, but he'd been doing a lousy job of it lately. Nonetheless, as he drove down the last block toward their home, Josh was flush with optimism. He'd learned a lot this weekend. As he expected, it was just what he'd needed, and he was ready to hit the ground running first thing in the morning.

Instead, he found himself hitting the brakes.

Josh jerked against the seatbelt, and was dimly aware that his success journal had slid off the seat to the floor. He stared ahead, his brain working to process what he was seeing. His headlights illuminated the lawn of the house next to his. It was the home of Ben and Alexa Halton—great neighbors, and better yet, great friends. It was something he and Kiera were both grateful for. In a teeming sea of people going about their lives, they'd found a truly wonderful friendship right next door. Josh stared through the windshield at the Haltons' house, and there staring back at him, in the glow of his headlights, was a sign. *A real estate sign*. The Haltons were selling their home.

Josh finally put the car in gear and pulled ahead the short distance to his driveway. He shut the engine off, then looked again at the sign next door and shook his head in disbelief. He just sat there, looking through the windshield.

He wasn't shocked that they were selling their home. The truth was, they'd been talking about it for a while. They weren't moving far, Josh knew—just a few blocks over to get some more space. Their friendship would easily survive.

The problem was the sign. It wasn't Josh's. They hadn't picked *him* to sell their home. How could that be? In all their conversations about real estate—and he and Ben had had many—it had never occurred to him that they wouldn't list their home with him. And to make things worse, the person they'd chosen for the job, which Josh saw as rightfully his, was his nemesis.

Josh slipped quietly into his own home, and made his way to the bedroom. He sat down on the bed and pulled his socks off, flinging them one at a time against the far wall. He lay back on the bed and stared at the ceiling. Kiera stirred, then drowsily flopped an arm across his chest.

"Good seminar?" she mumbled.

"Yeah. Sure."

"That's nice."

Josh stared up at the ceiling. Why would they have chosen someone else? He just couldn't figure it out.

"Kiera?"

"Mmmmm?"

"Did Alexa . . . did she say . . . ?"

"Hmmm?"

"Never mind. Get some sleep."

"Mmm . . . okay. Did you put the mortgage money in?"

Damn! He'd forgotten! Their checking account was already at the limit of overdraft—stuck at the minus few thousand dollars that had somehow become the norm for them—and he was supposed to transfer money from his business account to cover the mortgage. He'd forgotten. Now they'd bounce the payment, pay a service charge, and put yet another ding in their already battered credit record.

And of course, *forgot* wasn't really how it had played out. The truth was that the money in his business account just wasn't *there*. He'd been counting on a deal firming up so he could get an advance on the commission before it closed. It hadn't. And although Kiera didn't know, he'd already spent the mortgage money on the sales seminar.

Worse still, Josh had been living off commission advances for the last eighteen months—paying interest and fees, and digging an even deeper hole.

Told you, said the voice.

"Shut up," Josh whispered aloud.

"Mmmmm?" Kiera mumbled.

"Nothing, honey."

Nothing at all.

Chapter 2

The Nemesis

When Josh woke up the next morning, Kiera was already out of bed. He rolled over and looked at the clock, then groaned. He'd overslept.

He gulped down a cup of not-so-fresh coffee in the kitchen, grabbed his things, and headed out to the car. As he expected, the for-sale sign was still on the Haltons' front yard. On the bright side, though, Ben had already gone to work. Josh wasn't sure he was ready to face him yet.

As it turned out, that would be the last of the good news of the morning.

Things started going downhill on the way to work. Josh passed three more new for-sale signs on homes, each with the same name as the one on the Haltons' lawn: Amy Deerham.

How is she doing it? Josh wondered. She seemed to be everywhere. At a time when nearly everyone seemed to be struggling in work and business, Amy Deerham was flying high. If anything, though, the signs served one purpose: They fed Josh's competitive spirit and he vowed to step up his game. He may have got off to a late start that morning, but there was plenty of day left and he had some big plans. *Look out Amy Deerham. There's a new Josh in town.*

When Josh reached the office he said a quick hello to Kelli at reception, then headed straight for his desk. It was time to get to work. He'd barely dropped into his chair, though, when his boss, Carl, knocked on the open door. "Can I talk to you for a second, Josh?"

"Sure," Josh said absently, as he rifled through a stack of folders on his desk. "What's up?"

"Come on down to my office for a few minutes."

Josh stopped rifling and looked up, but Carl was already on his way down the hall. He was a notoriously straight shooter, Josh knew, but a private conversation in his office? That meant a whole new level of forthright discussion. This couldn't be good.

And it wasn't.

"You're telling me I have to *leave?*" Josh asked in disbelief.

"No, I'm not, Josh. I'm telling you that there's not enough business coming in, and my costs keep climbing. You know the whole industry is changing. I can't keep doing business the same way forever."

"So what *are* you telling me?"

"I'm telling you I need to make changes. I don't pay you a salary, but all this office space is killing me. Filling a building with anyone who has a business card in the hopes they'll drive some sales just isn't working. I need to lower my overhead, and surround myself with top performers."

"That's pretty much the same thing as throwing me out," Josh said testily. "I can't compete with some of these guys. They've got huge referral lists and heaps of experience—they've been at this for way longer than me."

"I know, Josh. I know. But the industry is shifting under my feet. I need a new way to do business or *nobody's* going to be here. That new way is going to be surrounding myself with the best."

Josh rubbed his face. The energy he'd felt coming into the office just minutes ago had vanished.

"Look," Carl said. "I like you Josh. The staff likes you. Hell, even Wendy likes you and she doesn't like anybody."

Josh smiled despite his anxiety. Wendy was the unhappiest agent in the place. And she did seem to like him, or at least dislike him less than she did everyone else.

Carl continued, "I'd love for you to be here. If I were picking based on personality, you'd be number one. But I have to go by performance right now, and number one you ain't." Carl's phone buzzed. "Look, I've gotta get this," he said. "You've got some time. I won't throw you out next week. But by the end of the month, I'm going to be making decisions about where we're going. And," he picked up the handset of the phone, "who's coming with me. I already know who's productive, Josh. So do you. It's decision time. You need to change my mind. And soon."

"Carl, the end of the month is only a week away! Besides, how can I be even close to number one with people like Amy Deerham scooping business from right under my nose? I don't know how she does it."

"Maybe you should ask her," Carl quipped.

"Funny guy," Josh replied. "I wouldn't call her if my life depended on it."

Carl looked at him for a moment. "Maybe it does, Josh." Then he shrugged, picked up the phone, and the meeting was over.

Josh sat at his desk in a funk. This was trouble. He and Kiera were already struggling. How would they make it if his business failed? How would he break the news to Kiera? He could always move to a new brokerage, but he'd chosen this one because it was the best. Just moving down the street didn't feel like a step up.

Finally, unable to stay in the office any longer, he grabbed his coat and bolted for the door.

Josh drove aimlessly for an hour, his mind racing. The thought of finding new work was daunting, particularly in these slower times. He stopped for more coffee, then stopped again. At some point, he realized his hands were shaking, and he put the second cup down, unfinished. He needed some food. Before he made it a single block, though, he saw yet *another* Amy Deerham sign. He stopped the car.

"It's like I'm being punished," he said aloud.

But then Carl's words came back to him.

Maybe Carl was right, he thought angrily. *Maybe I should call her. I'll tell her off for stealing my business. She should stay out of my backyard.*

Part of him knew this wasn't a smart idea, but it was a small part of him, and before he knew it, Josh was dialing the number on the sign. He was going to give Amy Deerham a piece of his mind.

■　■　■

A few minutes later, Josh realized he had indeed given Amy Deerham a piece of something. But if anything, it was his heart, not his mind.

Not only had she been gracious on the phone, but she was also contagiously cheerful and friendly. And she had suggested something that Josh couldn't believe: She offered to *help*.

He hung up the phone in a daze. *Was he crazy, or was she?* It had to be one of them. Helping your competition? For Josh it was unheard of. Or was it a scam? Maybe she knew he was in trouble and thought she could buy his meager client list. Or hire him as her gopher agent and take advantage of him while we was in a tough spot.

There was only one way to find out. Josh put the car in gear and headed for the address Amy had given him on the phone.

As he pulled up, he looked at the street, then at his map, then at the street again. He was sure this was the place, but he was parked in front of a retirement home, not the coffee shop or deli he had envisioned for a meeting spot. Autumn leaves tumbled through the air in the brisk wind that buffeted his car.

He was about to hit redial on his phone and ask Amy for directions again when he spotted her waving at him from the sidewalk. Even from the car, he could see the huge smile on her face. It was the same smile that had been dogging him from front lawns across the city.

Josh got out of the car, and walked toward her. Amy held a coffee cup in both hands. *She's a lot smaller than I imagined*, he thought briefly, then she nimbly stacked one coffee cup on top of the other, and took his hand.

"Hi Josh," she said brightly. "Thanks for sharing your time with me."

"No problem," he said, then felt immediately foolish. Shouldn't he be thanking her?

"Here you go." Amy handed him one of the cups. "I hope you're a coffee drinker."

Josh took the coffee, grateful for the warmth of the cup, but even more grateful for having something to do with his hands and mouth. He was feeling increasingly uncomfortable. *She's just so damn . . . nice,* he thought.

"Let's have a seat," Amy suggested. Josh followed her to the side of the building, where two small park benches bridged the gap between the sidewalk and the retirement home. Josh sat down, and turned slightly to face Amy. From his viewpoint, he could see several elderly people braving the fall winds to move slowly about the facility grounds on a paved pathway.

"You always meet at the old folks home?" he asked.

Amy grinned at him. "It's a good spot. Some great perks. Makes me feel younger, for one." She laughed at herself.

Right now, Josh just felt *weirder*, not younger, but he nodded and smiled back. As he looked at her earnest face, though, Josh felt an unexpected sense of comfort. And he found himself doing something he hadn't planned on: confessing.

"To be honest, I called to . . . well, to give you a piece of my mind. I've had a rough day, and I kept seeing your signs, and . . . " He trailed off. How do you explain anything to your mortal enemy when they're sitting on a park bench smiling like it's Christmas Day?

To his surprise, Amy's smile got even brighter.

"It was great that you called, Josh. Good timing, really. And eerie, too."

"How so?"

"I started in this business three years ago," Amy explained. "I struggled terribly for the first year. And one day I had a day just like the one you seem to be having."

Three years? She'd done all this in three years?

"Things weren't going that well at first, and I was becoming frustrated. One particularly bad day I did the same thing as you. I called a man who was . . . well, he was pissing me off." She giggled. "I realize now that I was just taking out my frustrations on someone else. I was prejudging someone I never met, and not accepting responsibility for my own results. But it turned out to be the best phone call I ever made."

Josh looked away, thinking back to his own prejudging. "Did he invite you to a retirement home?" he finally asked, to lighten the mood.

Amy laughed. "No. But we did go for a drive. And my life changed forever."

Josh was skeptical. "A drive? Nice way to spend an afternoon, but it doesn't sound life-changing."

Amy smiled. "It wasn't the drive, of course, although that *was* unusual. It was the week that followed—and, obviously, the months after that. But it was what I learned in that one week that changed everything."

"That's it? You called him up, and...everything changed?"

Amy grinned. "Not exactly. After I calmed down, I confessed that I was struggling and I resented his success."

"What did he do?"

"He laughed, in an *is-that-all?* kind of way. Then he...well, he *fixed* me."

"A guy who took you for a drive made you successful?"

Amy laughed. "No. I did the work. But he gave me the tools. And more importantly, he helped me *use* them. He helped me become accountable for what I needed to do."

Josh squinted at her in confusion.

"He gave you connections? Or... I don't know... referrals? What kind of tools?"

Amy turned to face Josh head on. "That's why I was glad you called. Do you really want to know? I mean, *really?*"

"Sure. Why wouldn't I? But..." He trailed off.

Amy giggled again. "But why would I tell you?"

"Well... yeah. Why would you tell me?"

"If you'd asked me that a few years ago, I wouldn't have known the answer. Now I know it's just part of putting the tools to work."

Josh didn't quite understand. It all seemed very mysterious. Was it some kind of marketing system? Whatever the tools were, surely she needed them to keep working, didn't she?

"I know this must seem strange, Josh. I think for now you'll just have to trust me."

This is getting weirder by the minute, Josh thought. But then he thought about his last 12 hours—the mortgage, the Haltons, the conversation with Carl—and decided that going with the flow was about the only choice he had at the moment. And, truth be told, he *did* trust her. He just couldn't quite put his finger on *why*.

"That seems very generous," Josh said. "How can I see these . . . *tools?*"

"Interesting choice of words. *Seeing* is exactly what you need to do."

Before Josh could even try to digest what that meant, she continued, "And to do that, we'll need to go to the source."

"Where's that?"

"It's not a *where*. It's a *who*. If you're serious, then I'll take you to meet the man who gave them to me."

This was all getting too strange for Josh. But at this point, what did he have to lose? "It sounds great," he said. "How do we set up a time?"

"Hold on. I should warn you. It'll be more than just a simple meeting. You'll need to block some serious time this week."

Josh's eyes widened. "*This* week?" He thought back to what Carl had told him that morning. "Of all the weeks, this is not the one," he said. "I've got some important things on my plate this week. I don't think I can do it." He explained the bind he was in.

Amy was silent for a moment. Then she turned to Josh and said, "Just my two bits, but it sounds like there's nothing else on earth *more* important for you to do this week."

Josh looked at her in disbelief. But she wasn't joking. He looked past her, into the grassy yard of the retirement home where a shawl-wrapped elderly woman was being wheeled slowly around the concrete path. *This is nuts*, he thought. *I can't spare this kind of time.* As he watched, the woman in the wheelchair looked up and a huge grin spread across her face. Josh didn't think he'd ever seen anyone so *happy*. And was she looking at *him?*

She wasn't. Josh nearly dropped his coffee as a small boy, no more than five years old, ran right in front of him, his arms and legs spinning like windmills.

"Grandma!" he yelled. "Grandma!"

The old woman's grin transformed even further, into an expression of absolute bliss, as the boy skidded to a halt, and climbed right into her lap. She wrapped her thin arms around him, and closed her eyes, burying her face in his hair.

Josh felt the wind ripple through his own hair. Amy's words came back to him. *Nothing more important.*

He turned to look at Amy. She'd been watching him closely. She smiled kindly. "That's the other reason I come here, Josh," she said softly. Then she turned to face the woman and her grandson, and sipped her coffee in contented silence.

Josh found himself smiling as he watched.

You just bounced your mortgage payment, found out your livelihood is in jeopardy, and you're spending time with the woman who just scooped your next commission check from right under your nose. And you're smiling?

He felt a small tickle of excitement in his stomach. Maybe he was crazy, but right now crazy was better than anywhere else he could go. He turned toward Amy. "Let's go see your friend."

Chapter 3

The Cub

Josh followed Amy's car as she drove to the outskirts of town. On the way, he made a quick call to the office to check in.

"Josh?" Kelli the receptionist ventured as he was about to say goodbye. "What's going on? This place has gone...bipolar or something. Half the people are walking like zombies, and the other half are racing around like the place is on fire. Which, by the way, it isn't."

"Talk to Carl."

"I'm talking to you."

Josh had no idea where to even begin. Before Kelli could grill him further, he said a hurried goodbye and turned his attention back to the road ahead.

Here I am, chasing Amy Deerham again, he thought, as he followed her dust as she turned onto a secondary road. No sooner had the thought entered his mind, when he saw her arm extend through her sunroof and give him a cheerful wave.

I'm not chasing this time, he thought. *I'm following.*

That, he decided, was both different and okay.

As they emerged from a tree-lined stretch of road and topped a rise, Josh realized where he was: wine country. Once some of the richest farmland in the county, it was now home to some of the richest *people*. It was a patchwork of wealthy hobby farm estates and small wineries. Even as he cleared the hill, Josh could see in one glance the orderly rows of several vineyards, the white fencing of riding stables and pasture, and at least one private airstrip.

For someone in Josh's line of work, just *driving* through this neighborhood was a dream. The thought of actually *working* in it?—of having clients here? That was the stuff of business legend. The sales and deals that took place out here created stars in real estate, and in many businesses, for that matter.

If Amy was taking him to meet someone in this neighborhood, then Josh's prospects were picking up indeed. *Of course, there are exceptions to every neighborhood. And apparently I've found one*, Josh thought as Amy passed the last large estate on the road, and turned down a gravel laneway that ended at a simple steel building. The daydream Josh had been having about the commission on a ten-million-dollar sale vanished into smoke.

The place was a dump. Everywhere Josh looked he could see rusting steel remains, the skeletons of cars, and machinery. Amy parked her car and Josh followed suit. They walked toward the huge open door of what Josh could now see was a large garage. As they drew closer, an older man in coveralls looked up. He stood up from one of the bays of the garage, where Josh could see he was working on a motorcycle of some kind. Josh could also now see that the interior of the shop was absolutely immaculate. It looked more like a surgical ward than a garage. *How strange*, Josh thought. *You'd think he'd clean up the outside.*

The old man—Josh pegged him in his late seventies—smiled at Amy, and nodded in Josh's direction.

"Cor. You're filthy!" She ran to him and gave him a hug, which he returned with enthusiasm.

"Now so are you," he said with a smile. Then he turned to Josh.

"You must be Josh," he said, extending a greasy hand. "Pardon the grime, but I'm delivering a baby over here, and sometimes that's work that you can't stay clean doing. Unlike real babies, though, I think I can put this one on hold so we can have some lunch. Sound good?"

Josh stared after the old man, then followed Amy and Cor deeper into the shop. Cor led them to a small folding table in one corner, and motioned for them to sit. Like everything else in the place, the tiny corner with the table was immaculate.

Josh sat facing the open bay door, looking onto the rusted piles of junk and tall weeds. He felt awkward and, more than anything, *uncertain*. He'd already wasted so much time and money on seminars. Was this just another one? *What am I doing here?* he thought.

They ate a simple but delicious lunch of wax-paper–wrapped sandwiches from a small cooler. Josh was anxious to understand what Cor could have told Amy that was so powerful, but the older man seemed in no rush. He ate his sandwich in small, steady bites, occasionally looking up to smile at one or both of them, but never saying much.

Josh tried to hide his impatience by looking around the shop. He realized there were a number of motorcycles in various states of assembly or reassembly—Josh couldn't tell which—but they all shared a common trait: they were *old*.

This place is like a motorcycle museum, Josh thought. *And so damn...clean.* He looked again through the open bay door at the rusting junk piles and long grass outside. Then he looked at Cor's greasy appearance and at the almost antiseptic interior of the shop. It made no sense.

When his gaze returned to the table, he found Cor gazing steadily at him with what seemed like a twinkle of amusement. "You like motorcycles, Josh?" he asked.

"Sure. I mean, I don't have much experience with them. But it looks like you have some real classics in here."

The old man nodded thoughtfully.

"And your shop is...Well, this is the cleanest garage I've ever seen."

"And the messiest yard?" Cor asked, a small smile playing at the corner of his mouth.

Josh felt himself blush. "They are very different. The inside and the outside."

Cor took a small bite of sandwich and chewed slowly. When he finally spoke, Josh was sure a full minute had passed.

"I suppose," Cor said, "what really matters is which you think is the most important."

Then, before Josh could digest what Cor had said, the man stood up, wrapped the rest of the sandwich up in the wax paper and placed it carefully back in the cooler, and walked back into the interior of the shop.

Josh gave Amy a questioning look. She simply smiled, then shrugged and began to tidy up the few crumbs on the table.

Josh looked at his watch, and felt suddenly anxious. *The week is slipping away already*, he thought. *I can't afford to waste any more time.* Surprising even himself, he followed Cor across the shop and said bluntly, "I'm sorry to be so forward, but Amy seems to think you might be able to help me with my work. I'm in a bit of a tight spot."

Cor stopped and looked at Josh.

"Josh, I'll tell you what I told Amy when we first met. What's between you and success—however you choose to define it—is one thing: what you believe. Much like this garage, it's the inside that matters, not the outside."

Josh thought for a moment. "I don't mean to be disrespectful, but...I think I know what you mean and, frankly, I'm not sure that it's helped me. I've heard—and I believe—that things like paradigms or belief systems filter the way we see the world."

"I know the old Henry Ford saying. It's in every success workshop I've ever been to, and trust me," Josh sighed, remembering his missed mortgage payment, "I've been to a lot of them." Josh swept his arm in a grand gesture, "Whether you believe you can, or you believe you can't—" he said, adopting an aristocratic tone.

"—you're probably right," Cor and Amy responded in unison.

Josh blushed. "Well, anyway, I think Henry was probably right, but knowing that doesn't seem to have helped me."

"Henry was a smart man. No question." Cor pursed his lips in thought. "But I don't think that little gem was a make or break insight for Ford, either."

"So how does belief play into it?," asked Josh.

"For starters, Ford was talking about believing in yourself. I'm going to go out on a limb and assume that you already do. Otherwise you'd be working for someone else, not yourself. In fact," he turned to Amy, "I bet you wouldn't be here if Amy didn't believe in you, either."

Amy smiled and nodded.

"What I'm talking about isn't about believing something new. If you believe in yourself, Josh, that's enough."

Josh nodded, but wondered if he really *did* believe in himself.

"What I'm talking about," Cor said, leaning toward Josh, "is what you believe that you *shouldn't*."

"That I *shouldn't?*" Josh repeated. "What do you mean?"

Cor selected a wrench from an orderly spread of tools on a nearby bench, then walked to what looked to Josh like the oldest, rustiest motorcycle he'd ever seen. "Beliefs are like tools, Josh," he said. "Using the right one is critical." He fitted the head of the wrench neatly on a rusty bolt on the machine. "The problem," Cor said, "is that sometimes we think we have the right beliefs." He pushed on the wrench, but nothing happened. "We think they fit." Cor tugged on the wrench again, but nothing happened. "But then we discover that even though they *seem* to fit, they're not getting the job done." He pushed again. Nothing. Then the wrench slipped off, exposing shiny metal on the head of the bolt.

"Or worse still," Cor said. "They actually make things worse."

"So...you think I believe some things that I shouldn't?" asked Josh.

Cor shrugged. He walked to the bench again and selected a different tool and a large hammer. He walked back to the bike, and fitted the new wrench on the bolt. Josh watched as he swung the hammer against the wrench, and the bolt loosened instantly.

Josh opened his mouth to ask what it was that he shouldn't believe, but Cor smiled and held up a hand.

"One step at a time, Josh. Come with me. I want to show you something. I'll clean up lunch," said Amy. "I think I know where this is headed."

Cor led Josh to the machine the old man had been kneeling before when they first arrived. Like the others in the shop, it was an antique motorcycle, immaculately restored.

37

"This is a 1958 Honda Super Cub, Josh." Cor smiled and ran his hand over the weathered leather seat and down the gleaming back fender. "I suppose it doesn't look like much, but I think it's bigger than its looks suggest. Much like many people."

"It's beautiful, actually," Josh said.

"It's also a lesson in success." Cor grabbed a container of wax and a soft cloth, and began applying wax to the already-gleaming tank and painted surfaces of the motorcycle.

"Soichiro Honda, who created this bike, was the founder of Honda Motor Company. He's been called the 'Japanese Henry Ford.' He was one of the most innovative and intriguing businessmen of the century. And," Cor added, "he was also a failure."

"A failure?" Josh replied. "It's hard to see Honda as a failure."

"It's remarkable how many obstacles Soichiro faced," Cor responded. "He failed as a race-car driver. He tried for years to perfect a piston ring concept for Toyota, even pawning his wife's jewelry to keep going. Eventually, his design was accepted, but that was just as the Second World War began, and Soichiro struggled to build a factory for his piston rings, even inventing his own concrete formula to compensate for supply shortages. When he finally succeeded, the factory was bombed not once, but twice. He rebuilt, but steel was in short supply and, in order to find raw materials, he had to salvage gasoline cans. He failed, then tried again, over and over."

Josh looked at the gleaming bike. "Well, it looks like he finally succeeded."

"You could say that. Henry Ford might get more credit, but this little bike"—Cor ran his hands over the gleaming metal—"Is the best-selling motor vehicle in history."

"You're kidding." Josh looked skeptically at the bike.

"Belief is a powerful thing, Josh," Cor said. "Soichiro had an unshakeable belief in what he was doing. He refused to follow the herd, and he never gave up."

Josh thought for a moment. *Is that all this is*, the voice in his head said, *a rah-rah cheerleading session?* He said, "So I just have to understand that success isn't found in the herd, and it doesn't happen overnight? That seems—well, a little simplistic, to be honest."

"Those are just a few aspects of the nature of success itself that you need to understand, Josh. The real substance, though, is *how you get there*. That's where the real problems lie. That's where most people have been sold a bill of goods."

"It sounds like there's a conspiracy out there to keep me from being successful."

Cor laughed. "I don't think it's that nefarious. But as a culture, we've come to believe things about finding success that simply aren't true. I call them Success Myths. Not only are they not helpful, but believing them actually moves us further *away* from success. They create a gap between our thoughts and our actions, between our dreams of success and the reality we find ourselves in."

"So, why do we believe them?"

"I've often wondered the same thing. Have you ever noticed that success is concentrated? That in many industries, about 90 percent of the value is created by 10 percent of the people? Most people are fooled by the Success Myths. As a result, most people do what most people do, and it gets them nowhere."

"But why is that?" Josh asked.

Cor smiled. "Much of it isn't mal-intentioned. The Success Myths come from well-meaning parents, teachers, and friends who just want us to be happy. At one time no one realized that the earth was round. It took time for people to understand the new truth, but in the meantime the belief limited our actions for fear of falling off the earth. Now people are realizing that there are healthier, more powerful ways to do business, but it can take time for the world to catch up with that understanding."

"So . . . these myths. What are they?"

"Ah!" Cor smiled. "Not so fast. Like success itself, the Success Myths take time to understand, internalize, and, most importantly, to act on. If you want to learn them, you'll have to commit to the process."

Josh thought about his looming deadline at work.

"What kind of commitment?"

"A week."

"A whole week?"

"Every day for a week. Seven days, seven myths, seven new truths. And," Cor added, "that's just to understand the myths. You'll need to learn to put them to work after that. You can't change your life overnight, Josh, but you can change your mind."

"And that's enough?"

"No," Cor said, patiently. "It's not. You'll have to act. *But success is an inside job, Josh.* Unlearning the

Success Myths, and replacing them with new ones is about *changing your mental state*. Without that, the actions you take will lead you either nowhere, or somewhere you really don't want to be."

"And that's...that's what you taught Amy?"

"I don't think I taught Amy anything," Cor said, with a smile. "But over the course of my life I've met a lot of remarkable people who have taught *me* a lot. They indulge me every so often by agreeing to teach someone like you. Assuming, of course, that you are who I think you are. And that you can commit to putting what you learn to work."

Josh took a deep breath. Realistically, he had a week to keep his job. Sure there was time after that, but if he didn't show some results soon, he was in trouble. Yet here he was considering blowing off a huge chunk of that week on a stranger and his friends. He opened his mouth to politely decline, but a voice inside him spoke up.

You know you can't make the sales targets anyway. What have you got to lose? If you're going to screw up, you may as well do it in good company. Josh looked at Amy. She was poker-faced. *It just feels right*, Josh thought. He looked at Cor, then back to Amy. *Maybe I need to follow my heart, not my head.*

"I'm in," he said aloud, exhaling. "When do we start?"

Cor smiled. He lifted a leg, and swung it down on the motorcycle's kick-start. The engine sputtered to life and settled into a smooth purr. Cor pointed at the seat. "Right now."

Chapter 4

The Future Myth

Josh immediately regretted his decision.

What the hell are you doing?

He stared longingly, almost desperately, at his car as they swung onto the driveway on the tiny motorcycle.

Today you missed a mortgage payment. Then you found out your business is about to collapse. Now you're clinging to the back of a 70-year-old man who's driving a motorcycle that's just as old. Would it be safe to say we've bottomed out, Josh?

Josh glimpsed movement out of the corner of his eye, and looked over in time to see Amy laughing at him.

Apparently not.

There was barely enough room on the seat for *one* it seemed, and Josh could only imagine how ridiculous the two of them must look. Cor, in his greasy coveralls, ancient leather helmet and goggles, and Josh clinging to his back in a mixture of fear and shame.

Oh God. Please let me die swiftly in a head-on collision instead of slowly of embarrassment.

By the looks of things, though, there was no way this bike was going to go fast enough to hurt anyone. Not with two of them on it, headed uphill. Josh had never felt more ridiculous in his life. Death by embarrassment it was, then.

To his surprise, though, Josh actually began to enjoy the ride. It was beautiful country, and the weather was perfect—just warm enough to enjoy the breeze as the bike hummed steadily down the road. With nothing to do, no ringing phone, no computer screen, and no one to talk to—he was sure Cor couldn't hear him over the wind and engine noise—Josh actually began to find the ride *relaxing*. For the first time in ages, and despite the day's chaos, he found his mind clearing. *I need to come up for air once in a while*, Josh thought.

A few minutes later, Cor slowed and turned onto another long driveway, and sped toward a distant home. Flanking them were row after row of green plants, and Josh realized they were at one of the vineyards he had seen during the drive to Cor's.

Cor stopped the bike, and cut the engine. Josh climbed off.

"Well, that's a first for me," Josh said.

"Well you're going to love this, then," said Cor.

Before Josh could ask him what he meant, a loud laugh rang out.

"You still pulling this same stunt?"

Josh looked over to see a tiny woman—well under five feet tall—standing with her hands on her hips, smiling broadly at the two of them.

"Eloise," said Cor, "this is my friend Josh."

"Josh," she said, walking forward and extending both arms. "Let me take you away from this old man and his frat house initiations." She shot a reproachful look over the top of her glasses at Cor. "You should be ashamed, making this man ride on that ridiculous contraption."

Cor just laughed. "Eloise, you can live in denial as long as you like, but I know you can't wait to take a ride."

Eloise took Josh's hands. "Don't listen to him. Let me take you somewhere sensible."

"Now *that's* denial if I've heard it," Cor chuckled. "You'll be wishing you were still on the bike, Josh. Mark my words."

As Eloise led Josh across the yard toward a large barn in the distance, Josh began to wonder again what he'd gotten himself into. As they approached the building, Josh could see that while it may once have been a functional barn, it was now anything but. There was a parking lot beside it, with several vehicles lined along the building's edge. Josh could see the windows had been replaced, and as they drew closer, he saw a sign that said Agents of Change, Inc., near a porch-like entrance.

"Have you enjoyed your visit with Cor, so far?" Eloise asked.

"It's all a bit overwhelming, to be honest," said Josh. "I'm supposed to be learning..." Josh broke off. "Well, I'm not sure *what* I'm supposed to be learning."

Eloise cackled. "Cor can be a bit cryptic. I think he fancies himself to be some sort of enigma. Once you get to know him, though, he's like an open book. At any rate, we'll see if we can make things at least a tiny bit clearer for you today."

Josh followed Eloise inside and experienced a moment of dislocation. Where moments before he had been standing in a farmer's field outside a barn, he now stood in a quiet, climate controlled, modern office space. Like Cor's shop, Josh realized, the outside and inside of Eloise's barn were very different places.

Josh followed Eloise as she crossed an open lobby toward the reception desk. Her footsteps echoed, and Josh's gaze floated upward to the high ceilings where he saw that the beams of the original barn still held the restored roof and ceiling.

As he brought his eyes back down to the desk, he noted a large sign over the desk: Today is December 19th. He felt the strange sense of dislocation again, and it took a brief moment for him to realize it was the sign that was wrong, not him. *It's mid-October*, he thought. *Looks like they haven't changed the sign in almost a year.*

That thought was immediately followed by the sense of doubt he'd felt earlier in the day. *How much help can these people be when they don't even know what day it is?*

"Josh?"

He blinked. Eloise and the receptionist were both smiling at him.

"I'm sorry," he began, "I . . ."

"No apologies necessary," Eloise said crisply. "Happens all the time. The sign is not incorrect." The sign is not incorrect? What is that supposed to mean? Before he could open his mouth to ask, though, Eloise was walking ahead. "Follow me please," she said, without looking back.

Josh looked to the receptionist, who simply grinned. "Good luck," she said.

Josh caught up with Eloise, who led him down a hallway. She stopped in front of a closed door. "Please keep your voice down while we visit this room, Josh," she said, and without waiting for a reply, she turned the handle and entered.

Josh could see they were in the opposite corner of the building from where he had entered. A huge expanse of windows let bright sunlight into a large open room that held more than two dozen people engaged in different activities. In one area, a number of people sat at easels painting. Against the far wall was a kitchen area where a man ladled soup from steaming pots into stacks of containers, while behind him two more people ferried the sealed containers into a large walk-in freezer. In the opposite corner of the room, a larger group sat cross-legged on the floor in meditative silence.

It struck Josh that even the kitchen workers seemed intent on their tasks. There was virtually no conversation at all.

Josh took all of this in within a few seconds, then turned toward Eloise. She was watching him carefully.

"Who are all these people?" he asked softly.

"They're our clients, Josh."

"Why are they here?"

"They're all addicts. Substance abuse of some kind—drugs, alcohol, or food, typically."

Josh looked around the room at the odd cross-section of people and activities. He turned his body away from the room to face Eloise directly. "Look," he said in a low voice. "I'm not sure what Cor told you, but I'm not an addict. I'm not even a workaholic, never mind an alcoholic. I think there's been some kind of mix-up."

"No," said Eloise bluntly. "No mix-up."

Josh opened his mouth, but closed it again. *Okay,* he thought, *I'm here. I may as well see this through.*

"Right. So they're all addicts. I guess this is a treatment facility of some kind. What are they doing? Drying out? Detoxing? Retraining?"

"No," Eloise said quietly. She motioned toward the door. "They're goal-setting."

With that, she simply turned on her heel as she had outside, and marched from the room. Josh was skeptical. *This isn't any goal-setting I've ever seen.* He followed Eloise into the hall, but as he left the room he felt himself deflate just a little. *Goal-setting?* he thought. *If I had a nickel for every time I've done goal-setting exercises.* Once again, he found himself doubting Cor.

Eloise led him across the hall to a smaller kitchen, and Josh watched her tiny frame bustle about as she prepared tea for them both.

"Disappointed, Josh?" she asked bluntly as she set the cups down on the table.

"I'm sorry—it's just that . . . well, I was hoping for something a bit—"

"—a bit more original?" Eloise interrupted. "Don't worry. This isn't the same old, same old."

"But I'm really not an addict. And that's not denial. You can ask anyone."

"Don't worry. You're not being committed to a twelve-step program. We look at goals a bit differently here."

"But I don't see the relevance. And I have to warn you, I've been to more goal-setting workshops than I can count on both hands."

"Excellent," Eloise said brightly. She set her cup down and leaned forward. "Please tell me about some of your most ambitious goals and how you achieved them. What did that feel like?"

Josh looked at her for a moment. Her expression remained unchanged.

"Is that sarcasm?" he finally asked.

"Yes."

Josh cracked first, breaking into a grin. "Okay. Fine. Perhaps I don't know *everything* about goals."

Maybe you don't know anything, said the voice in his head.

Josh ignored it and smiled at Eloise. "Could you enlighten me?"

Eloise smiled back. "I thought you'd never ask." She settled back in her chair and took a sip from her cup.

"Achieving goals is really about two things, Josh. The first is goal-*setting*. That's what the people you saw in the other room are working on. You can't achieve a goal if you don't define it."

"That seems pretty clear to me, but I have to say that's the most unusual goal-setting I've ever seen."

Eloise pulled a small card from her pocket, "Let's clarify the first part—the goal-setting—a little further." She placed the card on the table between them. Josh saw that it contained three blank lines.

"To understand goals, you need to appreciate that goals are about a *future achievement*." Eloise wrote briefly on the card, then turned it around to face Josh. It now contained a single word:

_____ _____ ***HAVE***

"Goals are about what *we want to have achieved*—whether that's losing weight, hitting a sales target, building a dream home, or saving for retirement. Goals describe something we want to have achieved at a point distant from now."

"That makes sense," Josh said.

"To you and I, sure," Eloise said. "But in order to set a great goal—to define what you want to *have*"—she tapped on the piece of paper—"you need to be able to envision something in the future. That's something addicts can't do."

"They can't?"

"Not as far into the future as good goal-setting demands. Some severe addicts are seeing only *hours* into the future, Josh. Days at the most. Their immediate needs are too demanding. What might seem obvious to you is far more difficult for people who struggle with addiction."

"So, what are they doing here? How is all this helping them set goals?"

"They're learning to see into the future."

Eloise smiled at Josh's expression. "I know it sounds strange. But it's really straightforward. Once they get through their physical withdrawal challenges, they come here. We teach them to look further and further into the future. You just saw a small slice of that. Remember the sign in the lobby?"

"Sure. You said the sign was *not incorrect*."

"Right. The date was wrong, but on purpose. We're creating a whole environment focused on the future. We call it *Future Focus*. We take care of every immediate need, and encourage them to be focused further and further ahead. The people you saw cooking? They're preparing meals for a week from now, and freezing them. Each one is dated, by them. The painters? They have to paint an image of their life months from today. The meditators? They're imagining their future selves years from now."

"How does that help?"

"The basic activities—like preparing future meals— help our newest clients learn to shift their focus a small amount ahead in time. They're not accustomed to thinking beyond a few days or hours. They're looking for the next drink, the next hit—whatever it is that their addiction demands. But as they progress—as they do things like paint a future several months away, or imagine their lives in ten years—they have to be able to ask themselves big questions. They have to ask, *what do I want my life to be like? What do I want to have accomplished? What do I want to have? Who do I want to have in my life? What does it look like?*"

Josh looked down at the paper at the word *have*.

"Okay. That makes sense. But I'm still not an addict. I really can see further ahead than a few days."

"Fair enough. So what are some of your future goals?"

Josh thought. "I try to set sales targets at work. And my wife and I have talked about what we'd like our income to be. And . . . " he trailed off. "There are vacations we look forward to."

She nodded. "Then let me ask you this: how many of your goals have you accomplished?"

Josh felt his cheeks flush. "Not many," he said after a pause. "At least, not many big ones. I do feel like I've accomplished many things, but when I try to set my sights higher, things seem to fall apart . . . " he trailed off. "You know," he said after a moment, "it almost seems like when I set goals and *don't* achieve them, that I feel even more unsuccessful than before."

Eloise smiled. "Cor never sends me any dummies."

Josh laughed. "I'll take that as a compliment," he said. "But . . . why is that? It seems crazy; I thought the whole idea behind setting goals was to help you reach them."

"That's the idea. But it doesn't work when you're missing half of the equation," Eloise said.

She reached out and turned the piece of paper on the table back towards her.

"You've been taught that the mere act of *setting* goals—identifying the *have*—sets great forces in motion to achieve them. That's the first part of great goals. The *setting*. There have been entire books written about this. An entire belief system that says that setting goals will change your life. The problem is that there's a trap there—a *myth*. We call it the Future Myth. If I'm the first person Cor's brought you to, then it's the first thing you need to stop believing; that the act of goal-setting is what makes things happen. It doesn't."

Josh looked at the card on the table. What she was saying seemed to fly in the face of what he'd been taught. "What about people who say they were inspired by a great goal and it changed their life?"

"That may be true—goals can be inspiring. And *should* be inspiring. That inspiration is the fuel that keeps us going. It's a key ingredient in any great goal, as you know. The problem is that it's *not enough*."

Eloise motioned to the card on the table.

"Typically, goals are focused here," she pointed at the *Have*. "We describe a future state—what we want to have, or have achieved. When you set a sales target, for example, one that you can clearly define, and see in your mind's eye—when you do that, you're here." She tapped the card again.

"And you're saying that's not enough?"

"It's only part of the picture. If that's all you do, then you fall victim to the future myth by thinking that *setting* a goal is enough to make it happen."

Josh thought back to his attempts to reach his sales targets.

Eloise continued, "What's missing is defining *what needs to be done in order to get there.*" She wrote one more word:

$$\underline{\hspace{2cm}} \quad \underline{\textbf{\textit{DO}}} \quad \underline{\textbf{\textit{HAVE}}}$$

Josh looked at the card. "And you do this with your clients, too?"

"Of course. Once they've developed the skill of defining clear *have's*, we ask them to answer a simple question: *What do I have to do to achieve that result?*"

"And that helps?"

"It does more than help, Josh. It makes *magic.*"

"That's no small claim," Josh said.

"Let me give you an example."

Eloise stood up and took a framed picture down from the wall and brought it to the table. "This is one of my first clients." The photo was of a strikingly attractive woman, standing hand in hand with a man on a tropical beach.

"She seems happy," said Josh. "What was her goal?"

"To lose weight."

Josh looked at the picture. "You're kidding me. There's not much to lose, there. That's like me wanting to earn $10 more a year."

"This photograph was taken after we worked together," Eloise said. "When I met her she weighed over 350 pounds. She was different from our addiction clients. She had a relatively 'normal' life. When we began to work together, I could see she could easily visualize her goal. She was passionate about losing weight. She knew how much and by when—in other words, she had goal-*setting* figured out."

"So what was the problem?"

"She'd had the same goal for a decade, and had gained weight every year. Not only was goal-setting not working, it seemed to be making things worse."

"So what did you do?"

"What *she* did, with our help, was reverse engineer her goal," Eloise said.

"Reverse engineer?"

"Yes. That's how we get to the next step," she tapped the page. "We work backwards from the goal—the *have* in the future—then what we need to *do* in the present to move toward it. That's the second key ingredient in goal achievement. We set the goal, then we need to set the *behaviors* to reach it."

"That makes sense in principle," Josh said, "but what does it look like in practice?"

"In her case, we asked a single question: *What did she have to do every day to move her closer to that goal?*"

"Every day . . . " Josh mused. "Well, I guess she'd have to weigh a little bit less every day, and then after a certain amount of time, she'd reach her goal."

"No."

Josh looked quizzical. "But . . . it makes sense. If she weighed a quarter of a pound less every day for months, she'd reach her goal eventually. It's just simple math."

Eloise tapped the paper on the table. "You're still stuck in the *have*, Josh. 'Weigh less' isn't a *do*. It's not an action. What we did was direct her toward *behaviors*. Things she could *do*. Using your answer, she'd just get up every day and step on the scale and look to see if anything had changed. That's more like *wishing*."

"What she did instead was create a list of key daily behaviors that were aligned with her goal. Things like walking every day for twenty minutes. Shopping for a week's worth of healthy foods each Sunday. Making a lunch for work each morning. Even things you might not think of, like saving a little money every day for new clothes that fit properly."

"Once that was done—which took some time—she had in her hands a list of small, repeatable behaviors to get from where she was, to where she wanted to be."

"Why the focus on repeatable behaviors?"

"The key to success is to *do* things. The trouble is that the Future Myth fools us into skipping that part. But at the root, every success story is one of action and persistence. It's about doing, and then doing again. Breaking down big, overwhelming goals into simple, daily actions or behaviors is how we achieve them. In your job there are probably a handful of things you need to do every day, over and over, in order to get where you want to go."

"It seems like there are a million things."

Eloise laughed. "There are. But there are likely only a few that drive your business, that help you find clients and drive sales. The ones that add up to do the *most* to drive you toward your goal."

Josh perked up. "So what are mine?"

"In sales, Josh, you probably know you need to have a certain number of leads, which generate a certain number of appointments, which, in turn, result in a certain number of prospects, who then turn into a smaller number of prospects, who then become clients."

Josh knew the protocol well. "We call it the sales pipeline or funnel."

"Right. Each part of the funnel is like a sub-goal to reach the overall goal of more sales. That's fine, but the problem is that even though you've defined the goals, *you probably haven't defined the behaviors required to reach them*. You haven't reverse engineered your goals."

Suddenly, the lightbulb came on for Josh. "In the case of my sales goals, all I did was define where I wanted to be in the future. Not how to get there. I didn't define the actions."

"Take it one step further," Eloise prompted. "Not just how to get there, but the *precise, repeatable behaviors* that will bring you right to that goal. *That's* what the Future Myth reveals. Goals don't just tell us where to arrive tomorrow, or next month, or next year, Josh. *They tell us what to do today.*"

The lightbulb in Josh's head began to burn brighter.

"Like making calls. Or setting appointments?"

"Exactly. Only more specific. Making *ten* calls every day is a precise, repeatable behavior that can drive you toward your goal. Setting one sales appointment each day before noon is a precise, repeatable behavior. It's something you can achieve, and it's guaranteed to move you closer to your goal."

"But why have I only been taught to *set* goals? When you explain it, it seems . . . obvious, really. Why doesn't everyone teach this?"

"This isn't the lost secret of an ancient tribe, Josh. There are many people—coaches, for example, or people like me—who understand that setting goals is really about setting *behaviors*. In sales and business in particular, where there's so much emphasis on the goal itself—the money, usually—the idea of setting behaviors has been lost. The goal-setting has become the means instead. If you want to get somewhere new, you need to focus on setting and managing behaviors."

Josh thought back to the seminars and courses he'd taken. He'd never *once* been taught to set behaviors *as well* as goals. "I like the idea of getting somewhere new, but every seminar I've been to seemed to cart out the same story about not being able to get from New York to Los Angeles without knowing where you're going. They put a lot of emphasis on the destination—the goal."

Eloise smiled and took a last sip of her tea.

"People often use that old goal-setting example about a road trip. That you can't get to where you're going unless you know which direction to head in. 'Define your target,' 'set your compass,' etcetera. It's true—you really can't get where you want to be if you don't know where that is. Goals are important. Critical, in fact."

"But what makes the destination so important? Why don't I just skip the goal part altogether and just work on my behaviors?"

"Ah! Great question!" Her eyebrows rose above her glasses, and Josh knew he had asked the right thing. "Without the inspiring goal, we can't change our *thinking*. It's the goal that ignites us. And *that* drives the change in thought that in turn drives our actions."

Josh flashed back to his time with Cor: *You can't change your life overnight*, the old man had said, *but you can change your mind*. "The goal changes how we think," he blurted out. "It changes us *inside*."

"Exactly! That's why the goal is still important. It changes your internal state. A great goal doesn't motivate us from the outside in; it *inspires* us from the inside *out*. The problem is that most people have been so conditioned to define only the goal that they're not doing anything at all to move *toward* it. They don't take the next step. They're not *driving*. They might research the route and buy a few maps and get excited about the trip. But until they put in the mileage every day, a goal is just that: a distant point they never reach. The undeniable truth, Josh, is that you can't drive from New York to Los Angeles without actually getting in the car and *driving*." And with that, Eloise stood up and took Josh's cup to the sink.

A few minutes later, she walked Josh outside, where Cor was waiting, wished him good luck, and turned to leave.

"Wait," Josh said. "What about the other part of the equation? We only talked about *Do* and *Have*."

Eloise smiled. "Today's only Monday. One step at a time." She nodded curtly at Josh, looked at Cor sitting on the idling motorcycle, shook her head in mock disgust, and disappeared inside.

■ ■ ■

Josh figured he wasn't driving to Los Angeles, but his wheels must have been turning when they left the property—he barely remembered getting on the back of the ancient Honda, and he had certainly felt no sense of awkwardness riding the tiny bike and clinging to Cor's back.

His brain was working. It felt similar to the way he'd been pumped up after leaving the success weekend, but it was different, too. Instead of being pumped up about fat commissions and increased business, he was feeling something else: *the drive to do the things to get there.*

Josh realized he was grinning. He watched the fence posts fan by as they sped down the road. He looked down long laneways at the magnificent homes, the expensive cars twinkling in the sun. He was sure he even saw what looked like a helipad at one estate.

How much money would I need for one of those? Josh began to visualize what his life might be like if he could take his business to a whole new level. By the time they'd reached the shop, Josh was like a coiled spring, full of energy. "I can't believe how simple that is," Josh said, climbing off the bike and stretching his back. "I feel more energized than I have in a while. I really feel like I can see my future clearly."

"The important things usually are simple," Cor said. "Remember, though, that success is about practical application, too. You need to put your knowledge of the Future Myth to work."

"Oh don't worry about me," Josh said. "I'm on it. I can almost taste my goal." He thanked Cor, noticing again the little smile playing around the older man's mouth. *I can never quite tell if he's pleased with me,* Josh thought as he got into his car, *or laughing at me.*

But when turned to look again, Cor had disappeared into his immaculate shop, leaving nothing but tall grass and rusted metal in the afternoon sun.

The Future Myth

Myth: Goals create success by telling us where to arrive tomorrow.

Truth: Goals create success by telling us what to do today.

Chapter 5

The Knowledge Myth

A s Josh soon discovered, the next steps were harder than he thought.

Josh had left Cor at the shop to be home in time to meet Kiera for dinner. He felt invigorated. Passing the estate homes on Cor's bike had inspired him—there was a lot of potential in his business. *I just have to get out there and go for it*, he thought.

He'd planned to tell Kiera everything over dinner, but when he walked in, she said offhandedly as she bustled around the kitchen, "I see the Haltons are selling."

Josh was sure he detected some sarcasm in her voice, and so he'd told her a short version of the story of his day. He downplayed the problems at work and didn't mention Amy, either. He wasn't lying, but he just wasn't sure quite how to explain Cor and Amy.

He wasn't even sure he could explain it to *himself*. It was difficult to articulate the strange calm he felt when he was around them, mixed with an empowering sense that he could do *anything*. Anything, that is, but explain it to Kiera. He went to bed that night feeling strangely uneasy. His unease only worsened when Kiera came to bed without even saying goodnight.

Nonetheless, the next morning he had awoken at dawn, newly inspired, and set out for the office early, ready to take on the world. Having committed a week to Cor and Amy, he knew he didn't have many hours left for work. It was time to knuckle down. No sleeping in.

For the first time in many months, his drive to the office was *pleasant*. The abundance of Amy Deerham signs no longer bothered him. Instead, he found himself imagining Josh Abrams signs on every corner. Smiling clients. Commission checks.

It'll be such a relief to have some more regular money coming in, he thought.

How much? That was a good question. He had a pretty good handle on what it cost to run his and Kiera's life. And he knew *that* because the shortfall was what had been going on their credit cards and line of credit each month.

If I could double my income this year, the pressure would be off. We could get out of debt, and enjoy ourselves, too.

Double his income. It seemed completely reasonable to Josh. If Soichiro Honda could persevere, couldn't Josh? If Amy Deerham could build her business up so quickly, why couldn't Josh Abrams? She was wonderful, but as far as Josh could tell, she wasn't any more special than he was.

Double my income it is, then, Josh thought.

It felt good to have a target in his sights. He did the math. Doubling last year's business, and dividing that by twelve gave him...well, a healthy monthly commission. *Wow. That really would change things.*

With his monthly target lodged firmly in his mind, Josh pulled into the office parking lot. Inside, he was surprised to find the alarm off, the lights on, and Wendy, the surly rep, already at her desk.

"Morning, Wendy," Josh said, pausing at her open door.

"Right," she said, without looking up.

"Um...how are things?"

"How do you think?"

"Yeah. I guess...well, I guess this whole thing kind of sucks."

Wendy looked up from her papers. "You think?" she said, scowling. "Seen the staff room yet? That oughta brighten your day." She went back to her work, and Josh walked down the hall to the staff room.

Across one wall, a large whiteboard had been divided into rows and columns. It was easy to see what it was: a ranking of the performance for the quarter so far for each agent. Josh couldn't help scanning the rows for his name, although he already knew where it would be. The top two spots were no-brainers. In fact, there were likely only a few spots really up for grabs—the first two were locked. He found Wendy in fifth spot. *She's a contender*, he thought.

He had to scroll considerably further down to find his name. Josh was undaunted. *It only takes a deal or two*, he thought. *I've got lots of leads. I just need to knuckle down and get going*. He put the board and its rankings out of his mind, and headed for his desk.

■ ■ ■

It was during his third cup of coffee and fourth game of solitaire that Josh realized he was in trouble.

An hour's passed. How's that income doubling going? the voice asked.

Josh knew he'd been procrastinating, and he suddenly felt deflated. He knew what he wanted—or did he? He'd been here before: pumped up and ready to succeed, but then deflated when the moment came to actually get to work. Josh looked up at the whiteboard on his own wall. The only work he'd done so far was to write on it in blue dry-erase marker. It was a number—his monthly sales target.

Josh looked at the number, then at the computer game on the screen in front of him. And he started to smile despite his feeling of disappointment. He reached into his pocket and pulled out the small piece of paper Eloise had given him the day before. He looked at the words *Do* and *Have*, and smiled again.

Goals don't just tell us where to arrive tomorrow, Eloise had said. *They tell us what to do today.*

It was simple, elegant, and powerful, he suspected. And yet he'd fallen for the Future Myth like some patsy in a carnival scam. He'd been caught up in the goal—his sales target—and was spending his time dreaming about what he'd do with his next commission check, instead of thinking about what to do *next*.

That was the problem, he realized: *What to do next?*

He didn't *know*.

Just as Josh was trying to decipher what his goal was telling him, Carl stuck his head in the door. He was carrying his jacket and a cup of coffee. "Well, look who's here bright and early," he smiled. "Nothing like a little motivation. Good for you, Josh."

Josh looked at the solitaire game on his screen and smiled weakly. "Early bird gets the worm, right?" He tried to sound convincing.

"Atta boy," Carl said.

Josh watched him leave. Then stared at the commission number on his whiteboard. *Goals tell us what to do today.* That was the problem. He just didn't *know*. He looked at his watch. It was time to meet Amy. Maybe she could help. He grabbed his coat and headed for the car.

Josh met Amy at a coffee shop not far from her office. She was her usual smiley self—or perhaps a little more smiley than usual, Josh thought.

"Did you enjoy your ride yesterday?" she asked with a mischievous grin.

"Yeah, yeah. Laugh it up. I knew you were going to say that."

"Seriously, though," she said. "How was day one?"

"Good. No . . . great. I woke up feeling . . . energized." He paused. "Yeah. It was good."

"What's the matter?"

Josh sipped his coffee. "I don't mean to sound . . . ungrateful. But . . . well, I started off strong, but it wasn't long before I was . . . " Josh trailed off, searching for the right word, " . . . stuck. I didn't know what to actually do."

"That must have been disheartening."

"To be honest, yes. I mean, I've been there before. You think you've found a magic bullet, you get all excited, but then you're right back where you started."

"I know just what you mean, Josh."

Josh laughed. "Right. Judging by the number of your signs I see around, it seems like you know *exactly* what to do. That's my problem. I don't know what to do."

"I can't complain. I'm very happy with my progress. But I was in the same position as you once. And the first thing I learned was that there really are no magic bullets. The secret to success is there is no secret to success. There are just a few simple principles, practiced with consistency over time. You learned one of those principles yesterday."

"The Future Myth?"

"Right. Tell me what that principle says."

Josh thought for a moment. "Goals don't just tell us where to arrive tomorrow, they tell us what to do today."

"Right. So tell me what happened yesterday."

"Well, I got to thinking about goals. I got pretty fired up being around people like you and Cor—and around all those wealthy estates, to be honest—and I started thinking about how doubling my income would really make a difference for us. And I looked at that number, and it seemed...doable. Realistic. I felt confident. But I knew I'd have to get to work *today*, to make it happen, to reach the goal. So, I got up early, and headed to work..." He trailed off again. "...and then I got stuck. It didn't work for me.

I didn't know what to do next. Maybe the principles only work for some people."

"That, I can tell you isn't true. They work for everyone, always. There are no exceptions. As long as you set behaviors that align with your goals, this *will* work."

"So why am I stuck?"

"Let me ask you this: What did your goal tell you to do *today?*"

Josh thought. "Work harder?"

"Be more specific."

Josh paused, uncertain. "I guess I didn't grasp the Future Myth as well as I thought."

"We're in the same business, Josh," Amy said. "So, I can help a bit here. We make our money from commissions on sales, right? That's what your goal represents."

"Right."

"So where do sales come from?"

"From... offers, I suppose. Offers to buy a home. Without the offer, there's no deal."

"And where do offers come from?"

Josh began to see the pattern.

"From listings I have, or from showing other listings to people."

"And where do those come from?"

"From leads," Josh said, and then he took the lead himself. "And the leads come from calls, networking, advertising, writing, referrals, open houses, past clients, prospecting, and more."

"And...?" Amy made a rolling *keep going* gesture with her hands.

I'm watching a sale happen in reverse. From the happy client all the way back to ... Josh smiled. "I see where you're going with this. If I need three sales per month, for example, then I need to have a certain number of listings. To do that, I need to have a certain number of listing presentations." Josh closed his eyes and began to see the sales process running backwards like a film in reverse. "To get those presentations," he said, "I need people to speak with—prospects. To find them, I need leads. Those will come from a certain number of phone calls, meetings, etcetera." He opened his eyes. "*Those* are the things I need to do."

"Right. The calls, the events, the follow-ups. Those are *behaviors*. And the end result?" Amy prompted.

"I hit my target."

"Now tell me your daily, repeatable behaviors, Josh," Amy persisted. "What action is your goal telling you to take?"

Josh thought, then began to scribble rapidly on a napkin from the stack on their table:

- Connect with five new prospects each day.
- Make five follow-up phone calls every day.
- Set one face-to-face buyer or seller appointment every week.

Josh passed the list to Amy and said, "This is what drives my business." Amy scanned the list and nodded. "That's doable. The trick with daily, repeatable behaviors is to create a list that you can truly *do*. Consistently."

Josh thought for a moment more. "Okay. So, The Future Myth has just taught me what I need to do now. But I already do the stuff on this list: the calls, the networking, the appointments." He pushed the napkin away. "To be honest, Amy, I don't think that's my problem. I think I need to know what *else* to do. I just don't know as much as you—I need to do what you're doing. *That's* what's missing. You clearly know something I don't."

Amy looked at him for a moment, as if trying to make a decision. "Okay," she said, finally. "Let's go find your missing knowledge."

■ ■ ■

At first, Josh thought they were lost. Amy directed him to a part of town that Josh seldom visited. Property values were low. Crime was high. It wasn't high on his list of places to go looking for business. They stopped in front of a somewhat dilapidated building. Josh looked more closely and realized it was actually a *school*.

"Here we are," Amy said brightly.

Josh looked at her, but she was already stepping out of the car and heading for the entrance. He shook his head, and got out of the car and followed. Inside, the place wasn't as dilapidated as Josh had thought. *Like Cor's shop*, came the fleeting thought.

Their footsteps echoed down the hall, and Josh could hear the sounds of kids and teachers from behind closed doors. Josh wondered how an inner-city school was going to help him find his missing knowledge.

Amy stopped and peered through the window of each door they passed, then finally smiled. "Here we go." She knocked lightly and pushed open the door into a classroom. The desks were empty, but as Josh scanned the room, a woman looked up from a table at the front of the class. "Josh, I'd like you meet Anna. Anna runs a special program for adults here."

Anna was a tall, willowy woman with an enormous mouth that got even larger as she approached Josh with a huge smile and outstretched arms, and clasped his hands tightly. "Welcome, Josh. Any friend of Amy's is a friend of mine."

Josh still had no idea why they were there, but he asked politely, "You're a teacher, Anna?"

"Well. You could say I'm a teacher by profession. But," she laughed brightly, "they ran me out of that job a long time ago. I landed here—still at a school, mind you, but one where they are more...aligned with my philosophy, let's say." She winked at Amy. "But...that's why *I'm* here, Josh," she said, her large mouth smiling even more broadly. "What are *you* doing here?"

"I was kind of hoping you could tell me that."

"Josh. In my line of work, we don't settle for lame answers like that. Do better."

Josh stared at her for a moment, and then realized his mouth was hanging open a little.

"So. Why are you here?" she repeated.

Josh had the distinct feeling he'd forgotten to do his homework. He looked at Amy for help, but saw her trying to cover a smirk. As with the motorcycle experience, she was clearly enjoying herself. He was on his own for this one.

"I . . . " he began. Then he blurted, "I'm struggling at work, and I need to learn more about what to do so that I can grow my business, and Amy brought me to you, only I'm not sure why and so I'm hoping you can help, but I'm not sure exactly how you can."

Anna pursed her lips. "Okay. Breathe, Josh. That's better, at least. You tried."

Josh was beginning to feel like he was back in the third grade.

"Tell me, Josh. What exactly is it you feel you need to know? If you're here with Amy, that tells me that you've had a visit with Eloise already, and you know that goals tell you what to do."

Josh thought for a moment.

"But...I know how to do those things. And they haven't worked for me."

"So. The things that would help you reach your goal. You know how to do them?"

Josh laughed. "I've been to enough training and seminars that I could probably teach you how to do them."

"Then let me ask you this, Josh. Are you doing them?"

Josh's mouth clamped shut.

She watched Josh's expression closely, then turned and walked from the room. "Come with me please."

Josh felt a bit dazed as he followed Anna down the hall. He'd never met someone so...direct. All of his sales training and experience had been in very supportive, positive, rah-rah environments. This wasn't negative, to be sure, *but* the voice in his head said, *She nailed it, didn't she? You haven't actually been* doing *the work, have you? You told Amy you were doing it, but you really aren't.*

He thought back over the previous few weeks. How much.had he really done? Certainly, he'd made a few calls.

But you're not exactly consistent, are you? the voice said. *Unless you count how consistently you played solitaire and socialized online.*

Josh was grateful when his thoughts were interrupted by Anna, who led him into a room with about a dozen adults of various ages, busy in varying ways from working in groups in quiet discussion, to alone at desks.

"Pardon me, everyone," Anna announced. "This is Josh and he would like to know what to do."

Smiles and chuckles broke out in the group. Anna was clearly having some fun at his expense, and the class had obviously experienced it before. But the fun was well intended, and Josh felt himself smiling along with them.

"What should we tell Josh?" Anna asked.

In unison, they responded. "To read the sign."

Josh looked around, bewildered. Anna pointed behind her. Above the blackboard was a large poster. Printed in neat script was: The Knowledge Myth.

The Knowledge Myth

Myth: Success comes from knowing what to do.
Truth: Success comes from doing what we
already know.

"I know you're all very busy," Anna said. "Thank you for your time."

And with that, she turned and led Josh from the room.

Back in the class, Anna sat at her table. "Have a seat, Josh," she said. With no other option, Josh sat at one of the desks. "Let me tell you a tiny bit about myself and the students here. I started my career with a wide-open mind. I was excited to inspire students, to help them crave understanding and learning—to make a difference.

"My first job was pretty much the opposite of this place. A fancy prep school. Very posh. It was a dream job for a new teacher and I felt very fortunate. Within a year, though, it was clear that I didn't fit in.

"I tried several schools after that. Each was the same. I'd start with great hopes, but soon realize that all the schools wanted to do was stuff children with *knowledge*. It wasn't for me. I thought education should be something more.

87

"I drifted for several years, then by chance met a young woman. A remarkable woman. Bright. Very bright. Full of energy. Great with people. But she was stuck in a job she didn't really love, and worst of all, felt she had no choices. I was mystified. This was a truly remarkable person. She could probably have had any job she chose. As we grew closer, I asked her why she felt so trapped. Her answer surprised me: *I don't have a college degree.*

"I couldn't have been more shocked. That a woman so wonderful would be held back by a piece of paper simply floored me. The Knowledge the piece of paper represents is available for free in any library, or online. Andrew Carnegie saw to that. I knew that it wasn't the knowledge that mattered. It was *what you did with it.*"

Josh was spellbound.

"What happened to her?" he asked.

"I mentored her, I guess you'd say. I didn't know that at the time, but I encouraged her to shake free from the idea that the knowledge was the important part. That she needed not to know more, but to do more of what she already knew.

"The knowledge myth came from her. She took what I said and distilled it into that sign on the wall. She was, is, a remarkable woman, who's now a very successful and very happy entrepreneur."

"And those people in the room?" Josh asked.

"They're all referred or hand-picked by me. They're people who feel that a lack of knowledge is holding them back. As a result, they don't reach their potential. Our program helps them get over the myth of *knowing* and get on with the business of *doing*."

Josh's mind was beginning to race. She was describing *him*. All the seminars, the books, the courses. The *excuses* he now realized. He fell for the Knowledge Myth *all the time*.

"How do you help them get on with doing? I completely understand what you're saying, but," Josh thought for a moment, "I'm still not sure whether I'll actually *do* what I know. After this morning, I'm worried that when I get back to my desk, I'll still ... " he trailed off, searching for the right words. "I'm worried I'll just play computer games and push paper around," he finally finished. "I realize now that I've been lying to myself about work. I haven't really been *doing* at all. How do I actually *do* what I know I can?"

Anna looked at Amy, who stepped forward.

"Josh, I think that's best explained by someone who's had his own struggles with *doing*," she said.

■　■　■

The day was pretty much over by the time Josh left the school, and Amy encouraged him to simply work on setting his behaviors. "I know you're worried about actually *doing* the work, Josh. But trust me. You need to finish deciding what to do. Tomorrow is another day, and I'm sure the person we're going to meet will help. Just remember," she said, turning to face him. "Getting past the knowledge myth is about abandoning the fantasy of silver bullets. About feeling like there's some easy secret out there that everyone else knows that you don't."

"It does feel like that at times. Even right now, I still feel like you know more than I do."

Amy smiled. "I don't know more than you. Heck, I might know *less* than you. However I might say I *do* more of what I know. You don't need to know more." She poked her index finger at his chest, smiling as she punctuated each word with a sharp jab. "You. Need. To. *Do* more of what you already know."

"That's what I'm worried about."

"Don't. Tomorrow we'll find out what's holding you back, okay?"

Josh nodded, and he felt his spirits rise.

When Josh pulled into his driveway at dinnertime, though, Kiera's car was in the open garage, and he felt a sudden pang of guilt. *I haven't accomplished anything today*, he thought. *And the clock is still ticking.*

He took a sidelong glance at Amy's sign on the Haltons' lawn next door. And thought back to the sales seminar. *Maybe I should have thought more seriously about the coaching*, he thought. He knew other agents in his industry who had used coaching. He'd always chafed at the thought of someone telling him what to do, but after his day with Amy and Anna, he was beginning to see the value in being held accountable.

Yeah, said the voice. *Like the value in the fact that they're all doing better than you?*

Josh turned his head away from the neighbor's lawn, and headed inside, where he found Kiera in the kitchen. They exchanged notes about their day while preparing dinner together. Josh poured them a glass of wine, and was reminded of his crazy ride with Cor the day before. He told Kiera of his strange, but encouraging week. To his surprise, she seemed unenthused.

"You're spending your days with Amy Deerham?" she asked. "Isn't she your competition?"

"I guess she is," Josh said. "But—it doesn't feel that way."

Kiera took a sip of wine, then set the glass down. "I'm sure you know better than I do, Josh, but when I look at the sign on Ben and Alexa's lawn, she sure *seems* like competition. Nothing more was said about Amy over dinner. *But only because nothing was said at all*, Josh thought. They'd eaten in silence, and then Kiera had simply gone to bed without saying goodnight, leaving Josh alone with his darkening thoughts.

After dinner, he tried to shake his growing gloom by focusing on work. He took an hour to more carefully define the specific, repeatable actions he could do that would drive him closer to his goal. There were calls to make, appointments to book, follow-ups to make. Each one was clearly an action item, and directly linked to growing his business. Looking at the list, he felt cautiously optimistic. *If I actually did this stuff*, he thought, scanning the list of daily, weekly, and monthly actions, *I'd be a top performer for sure.* But it still seemed like a big *if.* Josh knew that there was a reality to face when he got to the office. He'd have to actually *do* the things on the list, and for a reason he couldn't explain, he just wasn't sure he would follow through. *Maybe I do need a coach,* he thought.

Fortunately, he was meeting Amy bright and early. He hoped that whomever he was going to meet that morning would have the insight he needed to move forward. Feeling hopeful, Josh headed for bed.

The Knowledge Myth

Myth: Success comes from knowing what to do.
Truth: Success comes from doing more of
what we already know.

Chapter 6

The Failure Myth

It was dark when Josh left the house the next morning. *Fall is here*, he thought. *The time is flying by.* That thought immediately reminded him of the whiteboard at the office and the few remaining days before the end of the month, and he felt a knot form in his stomach. It tightened further as he remembered that he had yet to tell Kiera the whole story about what was going on at the office.

To meet Amy, Josh took a street he seldom traveled on. As he slowed near the end of the block, he was shaken from his anxious contemplation by the sight of a woman in the dawn light carrying a sleeping child from an idling car up the walk to a home.

The woman was Wendy. Josh slowed, and saw Wendy kiss the sleeping child, and then pass her to an older woman at the house door. As she turned to leave, Josh could see the sadness in Wendy's face. She looked like she was on the brink of tears.

Josh met Amy at a park, and Josh commented on her apparent love of the outdoors.

"I just find I think better," she said. "Work doesn't have to mean a desk—at least, not for me."

Listening to the morning birds and sipping a fresh, hot coffee, Josh could find no fault with her argument.

"So you understood Anna's point yesterday?" Amy asked, after a few quiet minutes.

"Definitely. She's right—I really *do* know what to do. I just need to do more of it. When I really looked at my behavior over the past year, I realized that I wasn't doing much of what I knew. I was busy, but not productive, I guess."

Amy smiled. "Don't feel bad. It happens to all of us."

"But why?" Josh asked.

"The Knowledge Myth and the Future Myth share something in common," Amy replied. "They both make us feel like we're *doing* something. When we're stuck, or afraid, or uncertain, setting goals, and getting more information makes us feel like we're not standing still. The problem is that we often are."

"I just wish I hadn't spent so much on all those seminars, telling me what I already knew."

"Josh, that's always money well spent. You can never learn too much. And we don't retain everything—far from it. Continuing to learn is critical to reinforcing what's important. The knowledge myth doesn't tell us to stop learning. It tells us to start *doing*. It's about not being fooled into thinking we always need to know more to find success."

"Well. That's me, that's for sure. I've spent a lot of time *not* doing lately. A lot of time looking for the next magic bullet."

"That's part of the reason I don't stay in the office all the time," Amy commented. "I like to separate my doing time from the rest of my life. I've never been one to *do* 24–7, but if I carve out clear times for productive forward motion, and clear times for the other parts of my life, then I can get a lot done."

"I hope I can too," said Josh. "But I'm worried that I won't be able to. That I'll sit at my desk and still feel like I don't know what to do."

"You're not alone there either, Josh," said Amy. "That usually means there's something else standing in your way—something else you believe that you shouldn't."

"Another myth?" Josh smiled.

"Bingo."

"Then lead on."

■ ■ ■

Amy parked in front of a long, low warehouse near the city waterfront. The sign out front read: Methiant Industries.

Amy led Josh to a side door, and they walked directly into an enormous open space. It was spotlessly clean and humming with activity. While from the outside it looked like an industrial building, inside Josh could see the floor was covered in desks. The entire space was one large, open-concept office.

The place was a hive of activity, and there was a level of ambient noise of a hundred people at work, on phones, typing, talking, and otherwise carrying out business. Despite that, however, a voice boomed across the huge room, cutting through the background hubbub.

"Amy!"

Amy grinned. "No need for a receptionist here."

Josh looked in the direction of the voice, and saw a tall man waving and heading in their direction.

As he grew closer, Josh could see he was wrong. The man wasn't tall. He was *enormous*. He must have been close to seven feet, looking bigger with each stride.

"Nathan," Amy said with a smile. "I've got someone here I'd like you to meet. This is Josh."

Nathan stuck out an enormous hand that swallowed Josh's briefly, and then coughed it back up undigested.

"Great to meet you Josh. Welcome to Methiant."

"Thanks," Josh replied. "This is quite a spot." Josh looked at Nathan again. He looked so familiar, somehow.

"It's a bit of a nuthouse, but we like it."

"What is it you do here?"

"Well. In the big scheme of things, I like to think we turn failure into success. But," Nathan grinned, "most people call us a salvage company."

Nathan gave Josh a short tour of the large room, explaining to him how they monitored weather systems, marine radio channels, and stayed on call 24–7 to respond to distress calls and insurance emergencies.

"We've got teams of experienced salvage crews around the world ready to fly to wherever they're needed. If we're on our game, we can often save a ship and it's cargo. And when we can't, we can usually save the people."

Josh was fascinated. "How on earth did you end up running a business like this?"

Nathan laughed. "That's a long story, but let's just say it wasn't the typical route—if there is such a thing."

Again, Josh was struck by the idea that he knew this man. He just couldn't place him.

"You look familiar, Nathan."

Nathan smiled cryptically. "Maybe it's just my size. I was six feet tall before I even got to high school, Josh. It's hard to understand until you've been there, but as you can tell, I stand out in a crowd."

"No kidding. But at least you can see over everyone else."

"Well that's one upside, but there are some down-sides. When you're this big, people notice you. And they also notice what you do, or don't do. As I discovered early on, when you stand out this much, people expect more. More on sports teams, more on the playground, more everywhere. And when you don't meet those expectations, people let you know."

"That must have been difficult."

Nathan smiled. "That's an understatement. But I don't want to make this a glass-half-full story of troubled youth. The short story is that I grew up under scrutiny. I was streamlined into basketball—no surprise—and I did all right. I got extra attention, extra coaching."

Suddenly, Nathan started to look a *lot* more familiar to Josh.

"I was groomed for college ball. I was coached, scouted, and eventually got a huge scholarship—and more scrutiny. Eventually I was a number-one draft pick."

It clicked for Josh.

"Nathan Kensington. You're Nathan Kensington."

The big man smiled. "Guilty as charged."

"You *were* the number-one pick. You got a huge contract, and then..." Josh trailed off.

"...and then never played a game?" Nathan ventured.

Josh flushed. "I'm sorry."

"It's okay. I'm more than over it. I did what every sports fan calls choking. I couldn't perform in pro ball. Couldn't shoot. The day I signed that contract was the day I stopped being able to play ball."

"But why?" Josh asked. "You were amazing. You had it made."

"I was pretty good," Nathan laughed. "I knew how to play ball, that's for sure. But I couldn't do what I knew when crunch time came. From the moment I signed that deal, I couldn't take a shot. I'd stand there on the court. I could have all the time in the world, but I couldn't shoot the damn ball." He shook his head in recollection. "It still amazes me when I look back on it."

"I don't understand," Josh said.

"Neither did I at the time," said Nathan. "Neither did my family, my friends, my teammates, my coaches, or the fans. They gave me more training, more coaching. Then they gave me counseling. When nothing worked, they gave me a hard time. Then they let me go. It was over."

"But...why? Why didn't you just...play, like you always had?"

"Because then it was for fun. Once I signed, it... seemed different. The stakes were enormously high. In a word, I was afraid to *fail*."

"So, what happened?"

"I drifted for a while. Tried to stay in the industry, but it was too painful. I wandered, found booze and drugs. I spent time in and out of rehab. And then I had an epiphany of sorts. I was wandering the streets, trying to not stay home and not drink, and I heard the sounds of kids shouting. I followed the sound, and found a group of kids playing street ball. I stopped to watch, and it...it just hit me. These kids—maybe in late high school—were doing things on that asphalt court that only kids do. Ridiculous shots. Crazy moves. Stunts that no NBA player would ever pull. They were just having a good time and doing a little showing off.

"What was magical, though, was that I realized, *they weren't afraid of missing*. They were *doing*, without fear of failure."

"They weren't playing for stakes. They were playing for fun; and what that allowed them to do was . . . well, to do what I no longer could. To play without fear of making a mistake. They tried things over and over and over. And eventually they'd get it right. But I realized that not only were they not afraid of failing, but that *the process of failing was what was making them better*. I know it sounds cheesy, but that game of street ball changed my life. By that point, my NBA career was beyond redemption, but my life wasn't.

"The next day I started Methiant Industries. I had no idea what Methiant would do, but I knew it would do something, and it would find it's way there by failing forward. By *doing*. That's when I discovered what Amy would call *The Failure Myth*."

"The Failure Myth?"

"The Failure Myth is so common in our culture that it's like an epidemic."

"And you're saying that failure is . . . a *myth?*"

"Oh no," Nathan laughed. "Far from it. I definitely failed at pro ball, and many other things. I can tell you with painful certainty that it's real. What the

Failure Myth teaches us is not that failure doesn't exist, but that it isn't necessarily *bad*. That it's not the *opposite* of success. That, in fact, it's the path to *reach* it."

At that point, a young man approached and politely interrupted. "Could I get you to look at something, Nathan?" he asked, and Amy and Josh were left alone.

When Nathan returned, Josh had been thinking. "I can see how failure might put you on the path to something better," he said. "And I also understand that the pressure of millions of dollars and millions of fans would be enough to make someone choke, but I'm really not in the same position. I've got a few bills to pay, and very few fans to please."

"Don't fool yourself, Josh," he warned. "The only fan I was having trouble pleasing was me. You're under just as much pressure to live up to your expectations as I was to live up to mine. When I talk about stakes, I don't mean the money or the fame. I'm talking about our own internal voice that calls us a loser when we make a mistake. There's only one fan for each of us, Josh. And that inner fan does a lot of heckling. A lot of criticizing. And that makes it harder and harder to try. To take a risk."

"But I'm not taking any risks, really," Josh said.

"That's how we fool ourselves into falling for the Failure Myth, Josh. The fear of failing in front of your best friend, or your parents, or your spouse, is just as powerful—if not more so—than the fear of failing in front of a million faceless fans."

Josh thought for a moment. "I'll admit that I don't want to screw up, and lose my home, or be a financial failure. But wouldn't that fear actually motivate me *more?*"

"That's a great question. Fear of failure has its purpose. But it's not to reach success. The fear of failure will only take you so far. It'll take you to survival. It'll make sure you keep your house, pay your bills. But only that. It won't take you to the abundant success that you're looking for. Before you can beat the Failure Myth, you need to first acknowledge that the fear of failure is holding you back."

Josh thought about his own work. "You think fear of failure is stopping me from doing my work?"

Nathan thought for a moment. "You're in sales, right?"

"Yep. Real estate, to be specific."

"So...how many sales calls did you make last week?"

"Oh...gee...lots. That's a big part of my day, I'd say."

"So...how many?"

Josh thought. Then he felt his cheeks begin to flush. *A big part of your day, huh?* the voice said.

"I...I think perhaps I haven't been making as many as I could have been."

"Don't feel bad, Josh. Your not making sales calls is the same thing as me not taking a shot in the middle of a game."

"How so?"

"We're both afraid to miss."

Josh looked at Nathan and felt the truth sink in. It was true. There were all kinds of calls he could make, but he was afraid of being rejected. And not just calls. All kinds of things he could do in his business that he didn't because he was afraid he'd fail or was worried that he couldn't do them perfectly.

It's true, Josh realized. *The failure myth really was stopping him from doing what he knew.*

Nathan interrupted Josh's introspection. "It looks like the Failure Myth just hit home."

"Yeah," Josh said. "Slam dunk."

Nathan smiled. "It's like that, the Failure Myth. The idea that failure is bad, so pervasive, that when you see the other side, it can be a bit of a shock."

Josh was silent for a moment.

"I can tell you're not quite convinced," Nathan ventured.

"No. It makes sense, perfect sense. I really have been afraid to fail. But," he looked at Nathan. "I'm already wondering if knowing that is enough. What happens if I leave here and I'm *still* afraid of failing? Then, in a way, I'd be falling for the Knowledge Myth too, by assuming that simply *knowing* more was the solution."

Amy smiled and turned to Nathan. "See? I told you he was a sharp one."

Josh blushed.

"That's a smart question," Nathan said. "The best way I know of both to get comfortable with failure and also to see it as a means of progress is to *actually fail more*. You need to have the experience, Josh. You need to do the thing you're afraid of."

Josh thought back to the list of behaviors he'd worked on. The truth was, some of them were daunting. He didn't *want* to do them. "I don't know," he sighed. "I'm worried about being stuck when I leave here. It seems so easy when we're talking. *Doing* things successfully is another matter."

"Then don't," Nathan said.

Josh looked at him, puzzled. "But you just said to do them."

"And you should."

Josh raised his hands. "I give up. You've lost me. Should I do them or not?"

"You should," Nathan said. "In fact, you *must*. But," he added, leaning down from his towering height to get closer to Josh, "don't try to do them *successfully*."

■ ■ ■

Back at the office, Josh sat at his desk and did something he hadn't done in a long time: He looked at his list of leads. Or, rather, he looked at the list without passing his eyes over it as if the names didn't exist.

Josh had built the list carefully—friends, family, contacts, referrals, and any other name that was a remote possibility for business. He knew that that list was critically important to his success, and he tried to read it with fresh eyes.

But still, he did nothing.

Maybe failure isn't the opposite of success, Josh thought angrily. *But it sure as hell feels like it. Why can't I just do what I need to do?*

Then Nathan's voice echoed in his ears. *Don't try to do them successfully.*

At first, it hadn't made any sense. It had seemed like nonsense to Josh. But then Nathan had explained that focusing on a successful outcome was what created his fear. "Until you get the experience to do it right," the tall man had said, "you need to focus on just doing it. On achieving the failure, so you can get on with success."

Achieving failure. It was a strange idea. But as Josh sat at his desk, understanding began to dawn on him. *It's about learning*, he realized. *Not about right or wrong. If I just take action—make the attempt— I'll learn, and then I'll get better, whether I fail or succeed.*

Josh returned to the top of the list. He was willing to start at the top and simply work his way down, but there was a part of his mind that was looking for an *easy* call, one that might have a little *less* potential for failure attached to it. He skimmed downward, his brain processing, but he could feel his energy waning. Josh sighed. He just wasn't good with failure. He knew there were people who seemed immune to rejection, but he just didn't feel like one of them.

He thought back to the early days of his relationship with Kiera. Even then, he'd been too afraid of rejection to even ask her out. He had been so desperate to be close to her that he'd panicked and asked her *roommate* out instead. He cringed as he recalled his blunder. The roommate, of course, was no dummy. She not only rejected Josh outright, but had sat him down on his sorry ass and called Kiera into the room.

Josh felt his cheeks flush as he recalled his embarrassment. She'd outed him right in front of Kiera, telling her that it was about time the two of them quit pretending and simply go on a date.

And they had, Josh thought. And here they were, married!

I guess some blunders are lucky ones, Josh thought with a smile.

Then he stopped. Cocked his head.

He scanned the list again, running his finger down the names. His finger stopped and his eyes narrowed. He looked at the name his finger was pointing to: *Ben Halton*, his neighbor and best friend, the one who'd chosen Amy over him. Knowing they were going to sell at some point, Josh had added Ben's name to his prospect list weeks ago for a future follow-up. That, however, was not going to happen now. He was certainly not going to call Ben to talk real estate; in fact, he was unlikely to call Ben about *anything*.

How could they have chosen Amy over me? Josh wondered again. The sting of seeing her sign on their yard the night he'd returned from the weekend success seminar was still with him.

Some blunders are lucky, he thought. He looked at the list. *Failure* ... " ... isn't the opposite of success," he finished aloud. Then he followed the myth with the truth, *"It's the path to reach it."*

Josh tapped his pen on Ben's name on the list and picked up the phone.

The Failure Myth

Myth: Failure is the opposite of success.
Truth: Failure is the path to achieve success. ✓

Chapter 7

The Abundance Myth

The next morning, Josh, Cor, and Amy sat at a patio table at a small café. Josh was holding court, enthusiastically summarizing what he'd learned. " . . . So you see," he said to a wide-eyed waitress, "you can't just set goals and then expect them to happen. The goals are telling you where to go, sure, but they're also telling you what to do to get there."

The waitress opened her mouth to speak.

"But there's a potential trap there," Josh continued. "We keep thinking we need to *know* more in order to know what to do. We're always getting ready to get ready. That's a myth as well. Knowledge without action is useless. We don't need to *know* more. We need to *do* more of what we know."

The waitress opened her mouth, but was again cut off. Cor and Amy struggled to hold in their laughter as heads began to turn at other tables.

115

"But why *aren't* you doing more of what you know?" Josh didn't wait for an answer. "Because you've fallen prey to the Failure Myth. You're afraid to fail. You aim, aim, aim, aim, aim, aim, and never fire because you think failure is bad, when in fact it's the path to success."

The waitress interrupted. "My goal is to set down this coffee. I know how to do it, believe me, but my fingers are starting to burn, and if I fail, it'll be your lap that's on the path to success."

Cor and Amy burst out laughing. Josh stammered an apology, and sat back, red-faced. "I guess I was a bit excited," he said.

"It's okay. I was the same way," said Amy. "That's good news."

"So what happens next?"

"Do you think you have everything you need to move forward? To apply the principles?" asked Cor.

Josh blew on his coffee and took a tentative sip.

"I feel like I know where I'm headed," he began. "And I know what to *do*." He paused.

"You seem a little unsure," Cor said.

Josh thought back to his struggle at the office the previous day. "I tried to embrace the idea that it's okay to stumble," Josh continued. "So I decided to make some calls. Just...do them. And they went okay. I felt pretty good, actually."

"But?" Cor said gently.

"But I'm not sure what to *say*, exactly. It's not like I've never made sales calls. I just don't seem to be that good at it. I think I've survived this long on good fortune. I guess you could say, I know what to do, but maybe not how to do it. I'm not afraid of failing anymore. I'd just like to do a lot *less* of it."

Amy and Cor both burst out laughing, and Josh felt his spirits rise. "What I did realize, though, was that I was neglecting the most powerful part of the failure myth. That failure can be a *route* to success. So...I went back to where this all started," he continued. "To the night I got back from the seminar. I..." he trailed off, and looked at Amy sheepishly.

"What?" Amy asked.

"I hope you're not angry. But I called our neighbors. The Haltons? The ones who listed with you? And asked if I could come by to speak to them." Josh looked down at the floor. "I wasn't soliciting them at all. I just wanted to know how to improve. But if you're angry, I completely understand."

"Angry? Josh, that's fantastic!"

"It is?"

"You've truly embraced the truth behind the Failure Myth. You looked to a past failure to find a path forward."

"Well, there really *was* a path forward in the failure. Ben referred someone to me and I'm convinced it's because I was so open to learning from what happened. If it's who I think it is," Josh continued, "Then it's a pretty big opportunity. I have a meeting scheduled for Saturday." He looked up. "It could be enough to help me keep my job."

Cor smiled knowingly. Josh had the feeling the old man was never really surprised by anything. *He always seems to be one step ahead*, Josh thought.

"You still seem a little unsure," Cor said, interrupting his thoughts.

"Well..." Josh fingered his cup. "Going to see the Haltons was the right choice. It certainly got me past being angry with them. They were thrilled that I'd called, and apologized for not listing with me.

They were feeling awkward about it, too. So we got through that, and we're friends. No hard feelings. And, of course, I just got a lead that might change my whole career."

"It all sounds fantastic, Josh," Amy said.

"It does. But," he turned to Cor. "I really went there wanting to understand why they'd picked Amy instead of me. It wouldn't have cost more to use me, and we provide much the same service. When I asked, though, they had a tough time explaining it. So...I suppose to sum it all up: I'm feeling okay with taking more chances. Making the calls, doing the things I know I should without being afraid. But I feel like there's something I'm missing. Like with Ben and Alexa. I didn't get the sale, and even when I overcame my fear of failure to go back to them to ask them why, I'm still not exactly sure that I know. Now I'm worried I'm going to blow this big opportunity for the same reason."

Amy set down her cup. "What exactly did they say, Josh? Can you remember?"

Josh thought for a moment. "They kept saying that they felt you were just so interested in giving them all the help they needed, that they just felt it was the right thing to do."

Cor and Amy exchanged glances. Amy smiled.

"Josh. You couldn't have picked a more perfect way to start the morning."

■　■　■

An hour later, Josh, Cor, and Amy stood on the granite steps of a large office building.

This is more like it, Josh thought. They were in front of Welstood's, a wealthy private equity firm in the city notorious for its high profits and well-heeled clientele. *One client from this place*, Josh thought. *And I'd be set for a long time.*

Inside the building, a receptionist took their names, then ushered them into a private elevator. He turned a key and the elevator began to rise. Josh raised his eyebrows to Amy, and she smiled.

When the elevator stopped, the door opened, and the receptionist stepped aside to lead them directly into a vast private office, with glass walls revealing a stunning view in every direction. Across the room, a man looked up from a large desk where he was in quiet conversation with a woman. He waved to Amy, said a few more words to the woman, and she left through a side door with a large stack of paper.

The man got up from the desk, and walked toward them. "Amy," he boomed. "Cor! So great to see you. And you must be Josh. I'm Tyler Hastings. Welcome."

Josh shook the man's hand. He seemed quite young to Josh, but astonishingly confident, without seeming brash or vain. "First things first," Tyler said. "What can I offer you? Something to drink?" Tyler picked up the phone and ordered some refreshments, then motioned them to a seating area near the windows.

"Okay," Tyler said. "Tell me exactly how I can help. What can I do for you?"

Josh was taken aback. He was meeting with the CEO of one of the wealthiest firms in the city. It was already a favor beyond all favors. And now the man wanted to know what else he could offer? *And he seems absolutely genuine*, Josh thought.

"Josh?" Amy prompted.

"Sorry," Josh smiled. "I . . . wasn't expecting to be here." He very quickly summarized his predicament, and how Amy and Cor were helping.

"Well, you're in good hands, I can assure you," Tyler said. "Cor changed my life. I wouldn't be here without his help."

121

Josh was stunned. He looked at Cor and wondered again what secrets the old man in the dirty coveralls was keeping from him.

"The problem right now," Josh said, "Is that I don't seem to be able to close sales. To seal the deal, I guess. I don't have," he paused, not wanting to offend Tyler, "your advantages," he said at last.

"My advantages?" he asked.

"Well...one look at this place...and...I mean. You've got an amazing office, expensive clothes. Probably an incredible car. You can afford to really impress your clients."

"Ahhh," Tyler said. "I see. And you see those things as markers for success?"

"Of financial success, certainly."

Tyler turned to Amy. "A classic case of the Abundance Myth in action, wouldn't you say?"

"The Abundance Myth?" Josh asked.

"The Abundance Myth," Tyler repeated. "It's a common misconception, Josh. People believe that abundance is about *getting*. That success is about getting richer. Getting more stuff. Getting ahead. Getting the deal. Getting the sale. Getting a break. Getting a leg up. Getting it done. As a culture, we're obsessed with *getting*."

"Well," Josh searched for the right words, but came up empty.

"It's okay, Josh. You can just speak your mind freely. We've all been where you are right now."

Josh looked around and thought, *I doubt it*. "Okay," he began. "This may sound shallow, but I *actually do want to get*. I'd like to get ahead. To get the sale. To get more done. To get a lucky break. That's part of what success means to me."

Tyler smiled. "Look around, Josh. I think we can agree that I enjoy those things, too. Here's the distinction: I see those things as the end result of success. Most people see them as the way to get there."

"I'm not sure I get that. How can a beautiful office building worth millions be . . . the way to *get* an office building worth millions? Who would think that?"

"Well, to be blunt, *you* would. You just told me that success would be easy for me because I have all these things at my disposal."

Josh blushed.

"Let's use a different example, Josh. What are you driving these days?"

Josh gave him the make and model.

"That's a nice vehicle. Pay cash?"

"I leased it. I didn't really have the cash. Actually," he looked down at the floor, "I didn't even have a down payment."

"You can get a pretty fine car for half that price, Josh. Why'd you pick that one when you couldn't afford it?"

Josh felt his face redden. He'd never told anyone why. After an awkward pause, he said softly, "I wanted a nicer car than Amy."

There was a long silence. "Oh Josh," Amy said. "You must be killing yourself trying to make payments on that thing."

"It has been an extra burden I didn't need. But I thought the sales it would generate would more than justify it."

"So you thought *getting* a better car would deliver more sales?" Tyler asked gently.

Josh smiled. "I guess I did."

"The idea that we should 'get' in order to 'get' is probably the greatest problem facing our society right now, Josh. It's put millions of people in over their heads financially, trying to *get* the trappings of success in order to feel truly successful."

"I guess I can see that," Josh admitted. "We're in over our heads with our house, our cars, our furniture... everything. But to be honest, I do *feel* successful when I have those things."

"How do you feel when your line of credit is maxed, and you lie to your wife about your finances and you bounce a car payment?"

Josh's mouth dropped open. "How..."

Tyler laughed. "Don't worry, Josh. I haven't been snooping. But that's the typical state of affairs for most 'getters'."

Josh shrugged. "I guess I'm kind of average."

"No, Josh. You're not. But your situation is common. You have the potential to be exceptional. But not if you remain a getter."

"So what do I do instead of striving to get?"

"Simple. *Give* instead."

125

"And ... you do that here?"

"Josh," Tyler said, leaning back, "that is *all* we do here."

"Our whole goal here is to create abundance. We're not trying to *get* people's money. We're trying to *give more money to them.*"

"But don't you need to get their money so you can do that?"

"In a very logistical sense, yes. But that's not what we teach our people. That's simply a transaction. Our whole focus here is on *how we create abundance for others*. Not how we get their money."

"Just as the Abundance Myth says," Josh said.

"Exactly. The Abundance Myth says that we find abundance through *giving*, not getting."

Josh stood up. He needed to think. He walked to the window and looked across the city that lay out beneath him. "I'm not sure I quite understand. Do you mean I should donate to charity? Take a vow of poverty and give away my possessions?" He scanned the office. "That's clearly not what you do here."

"Not at all, Josh, although charitable giving is a wonderful thing. I'm talking specifically about doing

126

three things. The first is to stop thinking of material wealth as a *path* to material wealth. It might make you feel wealthier for a short time, but it's not sustainable. *You can't create abundance in your life by getting more stuff*. Does that make sense?"

"Yes. And . . . guilty as charged," Josh joked.

"Second, you need to see abundance as a *result*, not a route."

Josh thought for a moment. "So . . . in the same way I reframed failure as a possible *path* to success, I should do the opposite with abundance?"

"Right. You can't buy your way to success, Josh. It just ain't gonna happen."

"Okay. So abundance is the result of something, not the *something* itself?"

"Right."

"I feel like I'm missing . . . something," Josh joked. "What's the . . . something that creates the abundance?"

"That's the third point. To create abundance, you need to reframe your human interactions—both personal and business—as opportunities to *create abundance for others*, not opportunities to create it for yourself."

127

Josh looked around Tyler's office. "Okay," he said finally. "That seems to make sense in a feel-good sort of way. I like the idea of a world where everyone is looking out for everyone." Creating abundance for others. So is this a you-scratch-my-back thing?"

"Back scratching is scorekeeping, Josh. It implies a trade. That makes it just a transaction. That's not what we're about."

"Then how did you get *this*," Josh said, spreading his arms to encompass Tyler's office and it's spectacular view. "From giving?"

Tyler leaned forward in his chair. "Ah. Yes. That's always the sticky part for people." He stood, and walked to the window.

Josh waited for a moment. Tyler looked as if he were deep in thought, remembering something from his distant past. Josh looked at Amy. She tilted her head at Tyler and gave Josh a *go on, ask him*, glance with her eyes.

"So," Josh interrupted gently. "How did you accomplish all this?"

Tyler paused. Then turned back from the window. "Dinner parties," he said, finally.

Josh was about to ask exactly how, when a young man entered with a tray of food and a coffee carafe. They each prepared their own coffee, and settled back in their chairs.

"I guess," Josh said, to kick start the conversation, "You can probably put together a hell of a dinner party. Billionaires. Movie stars. Heads of state. I can see that you could flourish in that kind of company. I understand how that works." Josh sipped his coffee. He resisted the urge to add, *But I can't put that kind of power in a room for dinner.* Then he realized what he'd said. "I just fell for the Abundance Myth, didn't I?"

Tyler laughed. "You're a quick study, Josh."

"I built this not on dinner parties with heads of state, but with four blue collar families from the other side of the tracks."

Josh almost laughed out loud.

"I'm serious." Tyler grinned.

"Please," Josh joked, grabbing a cookie with a flourish and settling into his chair. "Do tell."

"You ever go to a potluck dinner, Josh?" he asked.

"You mean, where everyone brings something?"

"Right. Every guest brings a dish, and what you have for dinner is sort of a surprise. Luck of the draw . . . or *pot* as the case may be."

"Sure," Josh shrugged. "Plenty of times."

"Me too," Tyler said. "Not so much anymore, but I grew up in very different circumstances. And when we had dinner with friends, it was almost always potluck. Those dinner parties were where I first discovered *potluck math*."

"Potluck math?"

"Here's what typically happens. Ten people come to dinner. Every guest is responsible for bringing a dish. What invariably happens, though, is that *each guest brings enough food for ten*. It's sort of human nature."

Josh looked briefly over at Amy. She smiled back.

"And what you end up with," Tyler was saying,

" . . . is enough food for one hundred," Josh finished.

"Exactly," Tyler said. "It's potluck math. Or you can refer to it as Hastings' First Law of Food Multiplication," he joked. "And what happens to the leftovers?"

Josh thought. "I seem to recall going home with my share of doggy bags," he said.

"That's right," Tyler said. "And a full stomach, too. Plus the host always seems to end up with a heap of leftovers. We used to eat for a week after a potluck."

Tyler leaned forward and set his cup down.

"I brought that simple idea to work here. Everyone in this company has one job: *to bring more to the table than they can possibly use themselves.*"

"And the leftovers?" Josh asked.

"They're shared. And the host," he shrugged, "always ends up with a lot of them. That's why when people ask me how I got here, I say, 'dinner parties.' There's no doubt that I've done well for myself. But I got here by doing even better for others."

■ ■ ■

As they waited for the elevator, Josh still felt uncertain. *I'm a good person*, he thought. *I'm generous. I still don't really understand why the Haltons picked Amy over me.* The elevator arrived, and they stepped in. The doors were about to close when Amy stuck her arm out, and sent them sliding back open. A breathless man said "Thanks!" and climbed on with them.

"What floor would you like?" Amy asked.

"The lower parking," he replied.

Josh watched the exchange. It was the kind of thing that happened every day—someone running to catch an elevator. But he looked at Amy, and his mind began to hum.

They stepped off the elevator, and it clicked. "I know why they chose you," he said to Amy.

"Who?"

"The Haltons. I know why they picked you over me. Or, at least I think I do."

Amy smiled. "Why?"

"I watched you on the elevator. The rest of us were interested in getting to *our* floors to get on with *our* days. Not you. You were paying attention. You held the door for that man. You picked his floor for him. *Before* yours."

Cor, who had said very little throughout their meeting, spoke up.

"Her intention is different, Josh."

"Her intention?"

"What Amy did on the elevator is no different from what she did with your neighbors. Her intention with your friends was not to get their business, land a listing, or get a sale. It was to serve them. To help them achieve their goals."

Josh stood there, stunned. It was as if someone had just pulled back the curtains on some great secret. "I remember talking to them all the time about my goals," he said quietly. "About needing more business to pay my bills." He looked up at Amy with a pained expression on his face. "I never even asked them why they wanted to move," he said. "I didn't even give them my *interest*, never mind anything else."

"It's what they couldn't articulate when you asked them," Cor said. "When you do the right things for the right reasons—like Amy does—people implicitly trust that you have their best interest at heart. That's how an abundant future is created."

That's why I *trusted Amy right away*, Josh thought. "And not just the Haltons. Look at us now," Josh said. "I complained about how giving a week to learn how to grow my business was inconvenient for me. Meanwhile, Amy's given *her* week to help *me*, her competition, without batting an eye." He turned to

Cor. "You too. Everyone here is giving except me," he said morosely. "That's the common thread."

Josh looked back to Amy, who seemed a bit embarrassed by the whole thing. "I'm sorry, Amy. I never once asked you what *you* might need to do with your time. Or if I could help *you*. I'm ashamed of myself."

"Be proud of yourself, Josh," she said with a smile. "You just figured out the Abundance Myth."

■ ■ ■

Two hours later, though, Josh realized that, once again, he was stuck.

He'd left Tyler's office inspired, and headed straight to his own desk to put in a few hours before the day was out. *Gotta do more doing*, he thought. *And giving*. Tyler's idea of creating abundance, of giving more to others, had struck a chord.

As he looked out his office window, though, he realized he was *still* putting off what he *should* be doing, and he felt the same pangs of guilt and inadequacy that he had so many times before. He thought back to how spectacular the view from Tyler's office had been. His own small window faced directly into the grill of Wendy's car in the lot behind the building.

Same as ever for me, he thought. *I can't seem to break through. I need to give*, he thought. *To create* ↙ *abundance for others. But what do I give?*

Josh looked at the clock. *Another day was gone.* He'd again spent the majority of his day with Cor and Amy, and still failed to really accomplish much. *I do have that big prospect*, he reminded himself. *But what if I crash and burn with him? I hope this is all worth it.*

Again, Josh felt his stomach drop. He still hadn't told Kiera everything that was going on.

With a sinking feeling, he headed for his car and went home.

The Abundance Myth

Myth: Abundance is defined by what we have.
Truth: Abundance is defined by what
we give.

Chapter 8

The Value Myth

The next morning, Josh arrived early at Cor's shop with coffee for everyone.

"You practicing abundance, Josh?" Cor joked.

Josh blushed. "I paid for the person behind me in line, too. I do feel like I need the practice."

"How so?" Amy asked.

"I tried to follow up on some leads last night. I really was in a 'giving' frame of mind, but I realized that I didn't really know *what* to give. I wanted to focus on giving, not getting—on creating abundance for the other person—but I didn't really know what to do. Was I supposed to cut my commission? Offer to paint their house?"

"There's plenty of painting to do here," Cor said. "If that's what you really want to do. But I don't think a paintbrush is the missing piece."

Josh fidgeted with his cup. "Then I guess I really don't know how to put these principles to work," he said, exasperated. "I only have a few more days to make some serious progress, or what abundance I do have is going to vanish pretty quickly." He sighed, and slumped more in his chair. "Everything I've done so far hasn't panned out."

Including things with Kiera, he thought.

The night before had been a disaster. Kiera had taken the news of his work situation well. She'd been very supportive, and Josh was glad he'd finally told her. And that's when things went wrong.

Kiera had commented on how hard he'd been working, and how that was bound to pay off. But when Josh told her about Amy and Cor, her attitude had shifted. She'd been angry that Josh was wasting what little time he had—and with Amy of all people. They'd gone to bed without speaking, and Josh left early for work the next day.

No. Things were not going well.

The shop was silent. Cor finally spoke.

"I know what you need."

"You do?" Josh said.

"Yep. A ride on the Cub."

Josh looked at Cor skeptically. "Right. I've had enough rides on that thing to last me a lifetime."

"Then let's start working on your next lifetime. Come on, Josh. We've got an appointment to keep."

Josh watched the older man as he began to strap on his leather helmet and goggles.

This has gone far enough.

"No."

Cor looked at him, but Josh could see no surprise in his eyes. Perhaps a hint of sadness, but nothing else. The old man waited.

"I've given days to this already," Josh said. "I'm getting nowhere."

Cor simply nodded. "Fair enough," he finally said. "If I see any businesses that deliver overnight results without much effort, I'll let you know."

Josh tried to read the old man, but his face was emotionless. And then gradually, he saw a hint of amusement flicker around Cor's eyes. Then he felt his own mouth twitch in the beginnings of a smile. And then they were both laughing.

139

"Fine," Josh said. "Since I'm clearly an idiot, I may as well look like one."

He climbed on the back of the Cub, and they pulled away.

■ ■ ■

This trip on the Cub was the longest Josh had experienced. And, officially, the most embarrassing. Cor had driven them right downtown. They'd actually driven right past Josh's *office*. He'd buried his face in Cor's back to hide, then realized that he looked even sillier, and finally settled for looking stoically dead ahead.

Cor pulled into a parking lot and stopped beside a parking valet in a tuxedo. The entrance to the lot was lined with exotic vehicles. Many of them Josh couldn't even name, but he was positive they were expensive.

The valet stared at Cor, in his leather cap and goggles, and Josh clinging to the back of the tiny bike. Josh waited to be told to turn around and get off the premises, but the valet said something that surprised Josh more than anything so far: "Good morning, Mr. Berringer. Nice to see you here. I assume you'd like to self-park?"

"You're welcome to have the keys, Andrew," Cor said, with a mischievous lilt to his voice.

"Of course," Andrew replied.

"Over my dead body, son." Cor laughed. "We'll just park over there in the cheap seats." Cor pulled the bike up on the sidewalk near a Rolls Royce, then stepped off. Josh watched him, wondering not for the first time who Cor really was.

Minutes later they were standing at the back of a large room lined with velvet chairs. On the stage was a painting on an easel and to the right of that, a woman at a podium speaking into a microphone. As she spoke, people in the audience raised numbers to bid, and Josh watched with some amazement as the price rose, finally closing with a sale to a man in a row in front of them. As the woman wrapped up the session, she looked across the audience, and Josh could see her eyes twinkle in recognition as she spotted Cor.

Josh and Cor waited in their chairs as the room gradually emptied. Josh felt a tap on his shoulder and turned to find Amy behind him.

"I wasn't expecting to see you," Josh said happily.

"I wouldn't miss this for the world," Amy grinned.

The woman from the podium congratulated the buyer of the painting on the stage, then she walked towards them and embraced Cor.

"Melody," Cor said. "I'd like you to meet my good friend Josh."

She smiled and shook Josh's hand.

"Josh and I are in need of some insight," Cor said. "We're hoping you might oblige us."

"Of course," Melody said. "Although I doubt you need any of my insight, Cor. Why don't you come backstage with me?"

Melody led them behind the curtains where Josh found himself not in a typical backstage theatre room, but a long series of locked cages with the glowing lights of alarm systems. Several security guards stood at various entrances. "I suppose you know by now what we do, Josh," Melody said. "This is where we store items temporarily before they appear on the stage for auction. The actual long-term storage is far more secure and remote, but this works quite well for the transition to the stage."

Josh looked at the first cage, where a guard was covering the painting that had just been on stage. "That was quite a sum that man paid for the painting," Josh commented.

"Actually, it was a little low. By about . . . " she paused, "I'd say 8 percent. He got a deal."

A deal? The man had paid more for that painting than Josh had earned in his whole career. *And that was a deal?*

"How can you even . . . put a price on what something like that is worth?" Josh asked. "I wouldn't know where to start."

"Melody's specialty is value," Cor interjected. "That's why we're here."

Melody smiled. "Flattery will get you anywhere, you old charmer," she joked.

"Even into the safe room downstairs?"

"Well. Anywhere but *there*," she said.

"I had to try," he said.

"I wouldn't have expected anything less," Melody said. Josh had the distinct feeling that she and Cor had exchanged this same banter many times.

"Cor's dying to see what we have in the secure vault in the basement." She lowered her voice. "He might be the world's greatest salesman, but even he can't close that deal." Melody turned and led them from the staging area into a long hall, then into an open reception area. "Welcome, Josh. We can talk in my office. Can I get you anything?" A receptionist took their orders, and Melody led them to a spacious office overlooking the city street.

"Josh," Melody said, motioning him toward a comfortable couch in her office. Amy and Cor sat down, too. "Why don't you tell me what you've learned so far? Then I won't waste your time with things you already know."

Josh doubted this woman wasted anyone's time, ever, but he thought back to Monday, and began to summarize what he learned from Cor, Amy, and their friends, using the days of the week as a guide to help him keep track. "Well, on Monday I learned about the Future Myth—that the purpose of goals isn't just to tell you where you're headed in the future, but what action you should take *now*."

He looked to Melody, who simply nodded for him to continue.

"That made sense, but I was struggling with knowing what it was I should do. On Tuesday I learned about the Knowledge Myth, which says that we don't usually need to *know* more. We need to *do* more of what we *already* know. That was a big one for me." Josh continued, recalling the events of the week. "But at that point, even though I realized I knew what to do,

144

I also realized that I wasn't actually *doing* it. That's when I was introduced to the Failure Myth. I realized that I wasn't taking action because I saw failure as an endpoint—a mistake, instead of the path forward. ✦

"Once I realized that, I was able to take more action, but my success rate was still pretty low, overall." Josh paused as he thought, for the thousandth time that day, about his big meeting the next morning. "With one notable exception," he added. "Then on Thursday I learned about the Abundance Myth, and that I had to *give* or create abundance for others in order to *receive*." Now that he was running through myths in order, Josh could see just how carefully crafted the sequence actually *was*.

"But," he looked at Cor who smiled. "I realized I didn't know *what* to give. And that brings us to . . . today." On saying it, Josh felt a flutter of anxiety in his stomach. Tomorrow was Friday, the last day to put numbers on the board. If he didn't nail this meeting tomorrow, he wasn't going to make it.

"Is something wrong, Josh?" Melody asked.

Josh sighed. "It's okay. Just been one of those weeks."

"Actually, to me it sounds like it's been a week a lot of people would kill for."

Josh looked at her, and smiled weakly. *I hope she's right*, he thought.

"Well," he said, "I do have a big opportunity tomorrow. I'm hoping you can help me prepare."

"Well, let's see. It sounds like you're struggling with just what to *give* to your relationships to bring abundance to others."

Josh shrugged. "That pretty much sums it up. Seems kind of silly, I know."

"Not at all," Melody said. "In fact, I may be biased, but I think there's nothing more important to learn."

Josh's attention level went up a notch.

"What you need to give your clients, Josh, I can sum up in one word: *Value*."

"Value?"

"Value. It's what everyone is looking for."

Josh looked around, then through the glass wall of Melody's office at the luxurious waiting area beyond. Everything was of the finest quality. "If that's true, then you've clearly created some value for others," he said. "I'm just not sure I understand how you've done it. You basically take other people's . . . abundance in the form of rare things...and exchange it for other people's...abundance in the form of money...and keep some of that abundance for yourself. It seems like you're...well, just getting."

Melody looked up at the ceiling thoughtfully.

"You're missing another piece, Josh. The things that make you feel abundant all carry some form of value—your home or your car, for example—they have *value* to you."

"But that's where I'm stuck...I understand that things have value. But I'm not sure that giving away a new television with every home sale is...I don't know. I guess it could work, but it doesn't feel like *me*. How do I give abundance to others?"

"It's the *form* of that abundance that may be tripping you up, Josh. Let's start with this: "*Abundance is a form of value.* Does that make sense? Your shiny car has value to you, and therefore represents a form of abundance. Follow?"

"Right."

"But that's the surface understanding that most people have about value. That value is simply more worth. It's more gallons for the dollar, more tomatoes per pound, getting the house sold for a smaller commission.

"That understanding, though, is what we call the Value Myth. The Value Myth is simple. It states that value is not, contrary to what almost everyone believes, just more of what we want or already have. It's not the baker's dozen, or the extra apple in the bushel. Those are forms of value, but they're *the lowest forms.*"

"There are forms of value?"

"Of course. There are three forms of value. Each represents a way of changing the *value equation.*"

"The value equation? This is sounding suspiciously like math."

Melody laughed. "Not really. But the value equation is where everything starts. Each of us is constantly assessing the value of things. When we're shopping, dating, interacting—each time we're assessing what something is worth to us.

"Much of the time, this is a subconscious process. But it's there nonetheless, and it's particularly obvious at times when we're making large purchases, such as," she paused and looked at Josh for effect, "a home."

Josh smiled.

"Regardless, though," Melody continued, "the equation is the same for everyone: it's the benefit divided by the cost. It's the *amount of benefit you receive for the amount you pay.* When you get a baker's dozen—say, thirteen donuts for the price of twelve—then you've received more benefit for the same price. Make sense?"

Josh thought for a moment. "Right. So when I get 50 percent off at a restaurant, the value doubles."

"Exactly. It's the simple formula that we're all applying in one way or another each time we make a transaction. What the Value Myth says is that most people think that value is just about getting things *cheaper*, or getting more of something for less.

"The truth is that we can change value in three ways. First, we can change the price. It's the simplest and most common way to shift value. It's what you do when you drop a price on a home listing to attract more buyers. The price drop creates more house per dollar, which can mean more value."

Josh nodded. That was one example he was very familiar with.

"The second way is to change the *benefit*. If you ask your client to paint her home, or remove some of the clutter, you're making the home seem more attractive—more *beneficial*—and therefore more valuable without changing the price."

"I understand those things. But what does the myth teach?"

"It teaches us that there's more to value than those first two forms. It teaches that there's a third form of value that is far more powerful than the other two."

Josh leaned forward, "What's that?"

"The Value Myth teaches us that the secret to increasing value to others lies not in *more* per dollar, but somewhere else. It lies in the *unexpected*."

"The unexpected?"

"That's our third form of value. *Unexpected value*. Let me give you an example," she said. "Did you buy your wife flowers on Valentine's Day this year?"

"Sure. I always do." Josh looked sheepishly at Amy. "To be honest, I pick up whatever looks nice at the gas station on the corner on my way home."

"And how does she react?"

150

Josh thought. "Happily, she's thankful." His face clouded. "I guess she doesn't seem...well...overwhelmed or anything."

"Why not?" Melody asked. "It seems like a husband bringing home flowers would be reason to be quite happy."

Josh considered this for a moment. "I guess showing up once a year on the same day everybody else is doing the same thing isn't...that *original*."

"Right. It's *expected*."

Josh smiled. "And what's expected is the emotional equivalent of the regular dozen. There's no... extra."

"Exactly! So, at the risk of turning romance into a business transaction, how would you increase the *value* of your next flower delivery? Let me give you a hint: Twice as many flowers is not the answer."

Josh thought, gradually developing a deer-in-the-headlights look.

"Amy. Rescue Josh, please?"

Amy laughed. "Josh. What's Kiera's favorite flower?"

"I don't kn—oh! Wait. It's . . . " he snapped his fingers trying to remember. "It's daffodils! She told me when we picked up funeral flowers once. She said they were much better than roses—" his face fell—"which is what I gave her last year."

"Excellent. So, remembering her favorite flower would add value to the occasion. Can you take it a step further?"

Josh thought. *The highest form of value lies in the unexpected. What was so predictable about Valentine's D—*"I've got it! It's the date! I should bring the flowers on some day *other* than Valentine's Day. Because the only way I'd do that is if I *actually cared and was thinking of her.*"

"Bravo!"

"And I could have the flowers delivered with an anonymous note . . . "

"Sure," said Melody. "That's the idea."

" . . . and the note would say to get dressed up . . . "

"Right—"

"And to look outside, where there'd be a limo waiting, and . . . "

"Hey, Romeo," Amy interrupted with a giggle. "I think you've grasped the idea."

Josh blushed. "Sorry. But . . . yes. I think I get the idea. There are three ways to increase value: Lower the price, increase the expected benefit, or add an *unexpected* benefit. The last is the one that is the most memorable, creates the most loyalty, and generates the most referrals."

"Wow," said Cor. "I think he said that better than you ever have, Melody. I'd say that justifies a trip to the vault room downstairs, no?"

"Nice try, old man," quipped Melody. "Not in your lifetime."

Melody turned back to Josh. "Do you have any questions, Josh?" but when she turned back, Josh was already standing at Melody's office door. "No questions—I've got some daffodils to buy!"

And, he thought, *some value to bring to a big prospect tomorrow.*

Cor started to stand.

"No. Don't get up," Josh said. "I'll take a taxi, thank you." Then he grinned, and was gone.

The Value Myth

Myth: Value is delivering more of what people want.

Truth: Value is created by delivering the unexpected.

Chapter 9

The Attraction Myth

The sun was just peeking over the neighborhood as Josh pulled out of his driveway and headed for the office. He was on top of the world.

As he planned for the meeting with his big prospect that afternoon, he thought of his *unexpected* surprise for Kiera the day before. He had stopped on the way home and picked up her favorite flowers.

She'd been cautiously thrilled. She was still upset, but the flowers opened the door to conversation. And in the end, he'd apologized for not telling her everything sooner. And she'd apologized for not trusting his decision on how to move forward.

It's potluck math, Josh realized, as he turned toward the office. *We both brought more to the evening than we needed to. And the leftovers are still in the fridge, so to speak.*

Josh was also surprised to discover how *good* he'd felt to bring the flowers home. And not just because of her reaction. He was pretty sure it had something to do with creating value, and doing it by *giving*.

There's something....innate about giving, Josh thought. *Something wired into us as humans. When we give, we feel good*. In fact, Josh felt great. And if this new deal went through, he felt confident that he'd impress Carl, make a tidy commission, catch up on a few unpaid bills, and perhaps take Kiera away for a romantic weekend—unexpected of course—to boot. And even if he didn't, for the first time Josh had the feeling that things were going to be okay. *I'm getting my mojo back*, Josh thought.

As he pulled into the lot behind his building, he noticed Wendy's car already parked near the back entrance. *Early again*, he thought, and once more his mind flashed back to the sight of her dropping her daughter off at sunrise earlier that week.

Josh slipped quietly in the back door. He didn't want to take any chances with Wendy putting a damper on his good energy morning. Today was a big day. He padded silently down the hall to his office, thinking he'd close his door, get some work done, and avoid Wendy altogether.

He had just put his hand on the doorknob when he heard a sound from down the hall. He listened... *there it was again*. It came from the direction of the staff room. Curious, Josh headed a little further down the hall. He was surprised to discover that his heart was pounding a little in his chest. Slowly, he peeked his head around the doorway.

The first thing Josh saw was the whiteboard. Someone had updated the numbers the day before. Little had changed, at least for Josh, but he noticed Wendy was dropping, not rising. Some of the more experienced agents had deals go through, and it was pushing her out. *She's falling out of the running*, Josh thought.

The second thing he saw was the source of the strange noise: Wendy. The tough, surly, irascible rep was sitting slumped in a conference table chair, weeping.

Josh slowly backed from the room and headed back down the hall. He made some noise—banged his office door and coughed—to give her a chance to regain composure before returning to the staff room. When he got there, Wendy was up and turned toward the coffee maker.

"Hi," she said, without turning around. "Coffee's almost on."

"Thanks," Josh said, as he sat down at the table.

The coffee machine gurgled. Wendy was still turned away. The room was silent.

"This really sucks," Josh finally said.

For the first time ever, Josh heard Wendy laugh.

For the next fifteen minutes, Josh had a real conversation with Wendy; perhaps his first, if he thought about it. He found her to be someone far different than he thought: strong, capable, and smart, but softer than he'd realized.

"Let me ask you something," Josh said, refilling his mug. "Why should we even care about this? We could both just go to another brokerage down the street, right?"

"You care for the same reason I do," Wendy said.

"What's that?"

"This is a great place to work. Carl's blunt, but fair. The people are good. If we can't make it here, Josh, what makes you think we can make it *anywhere?*"

That was it in a nutshell, Josh realized. *It's not just my job at stake. It's my whole way of looking at myself. At what I can do. What I can be.* Josh looked up and realized that Wendy was smiling at him. He didn't think he'd ever seen her smile. "What?" he asked.

"I was just thinking that," she paused, as if nervous, "that this was nice. To talk."

Josh grinned. "It was. Thank you."

"No. Thank you." She stood up and carried their coffee cups to the sink. "This is a lonely job, isn't it?"

Josh was stunned. He'd never really thought of it that way.

"There must be hundreds of us in this city. All doing the same job. Day in, day out. And it's like we never even *talk*, never mind actually working together." She smiled at Josh, but he could see the joy was already draining from her. Then she turned and left.

Twenty minutes later, Josh pulled into Cor's driveway, and could see the older man in the shop with his beloved Honda Cub.

Josh waved as he stepped from his car, and walked into the open bay. "I wouldn't have thought there was anything left to fix on this thing," he joked.

"You can never wax too often, Josh." Cor tossed him a rag. "Start buffing."

Josh began to carefully rub the glazed wax residue, bringing up a deep, rich shine from the Cub's paint.

"I take it she loved the flowers," Cor said, picking a tiny fleck of grease from the exhaust pipe.

"How'd you know?"

"It's all over you, Josh. You practically floated in here. That and the fact that you're about five hours early."

Josh grinned. "It turns out the Value Myth is good for more than business. Yes. Kiera loved the gesture. We had a lovely evening together, and it lead to an open conversation about our finances, too. I felt...very relieved after."

"Value does that, Josh. It opens doors, and creates opportunities. In this case, it was a chance to speak openly, but it can just as easily be a chance to further your business, too."

They buffed in silence for a few minutes.

"Can I ask you something?" Josh finally said.

"Of course."

"I understand the Abundance Myth. That you need to further the abundance of others in order to further your own, but...there's always more to give. More people to give to. How do you know when to stop?"

"Why would you want to?" Cor asked. "Why stop anything that makes you feel so good?"

"What if what you know you should give is something you don't want to?"

Cor stopped polishing for a moment. Josh could see he was deep in thought.

"Josh. These principles may seem simplistic to you. But they're profoundly important and very powerful. My experience has been that for them to work, you need to use all of them, and you need to trust them. If you *know* you should give something, well, then you need to decide really whether to trust yourself and the principles or not."

Josh continued rubbing the shining chrome of the Cub, digesting what Cor had said.

"Is there something specific you felt you needed to give, Josh," Cor asked?

"No...I mean...I don't really have it to give, so I guess it's kind of a hypothetical situation." Josh stepped back to admire the shine of the Honda.

"You've really done some amazing work with these bikes, Cor. I guess you could say you've really added some value."

"I like to think so," Cor said. "But restoration is also how I remember the value trap."

"How so?"

Cor pointed to some wax residue on the bike, and Josh buffed it vigorously.

"I might find a bike like this in a barn, or a storage container, or at an auction or garage sale. And if I'm lucky, I buy it for peanuts. Or sometimes for nothing. And if I'm lucky again, I restore it to the point that it's worth many times its original value. I add quite a bit of value through my labor—which I really do out of love—and my knowledge of the brand, and access to parts and suppliers.

"But in the end, Josh, I always remember this: *I'm only polishing Honda's idea.* He created far more value by seeing *what people didn't know was missing* and bringing it to life. You and I can only shine up his true value. That is indeed value, but not of the kind that Honda created."

Josh looked at his reflection in the Cub's shiny gas tank and hoped what he was bringing to the table that afternoon was enough. *What value can I give to my business?* he thought. *What's my Cub?*

"Well," Cor interrupted Josh's musings. "Ready to roll?"

"Let me guess," Josh said. "You're driving?"

Cor grinned.

"I was afraid of that."

■　■　■

Cor stopped the Honda Cub at an open, treeless crossroads. They'd been driving for what seemed like hours on the tiny machine, and Josh's uncomfortable embarrassment had shifted to a more physical discomfort. Cor shut the engine off, and Josh stepped off, stretching his legs and back.

Cor lifted his goggles up, but stayed on the bike. "Your appointment's at noon," he said.

Josh looked around. "Here?"

Cor pointed down the intersecting road. "There."

Josh looked in the direction he pointed and saw a low, grey building in the distance. He recognized it immediately. "Are you serious?"

"Don't be late. You'll only get fifteen minutes."

Josh looked at him, but the old man's face showed nothing. "Okay. Any particular reason you dropped me here?"

Cor pointed at the stretch of gravel where the road was being resurfaced. Josh smiled. "Don't want to get your baby dirty?"

Cor smiled, pulled down his goggles. "Fifteen minutes," he said. "Make them count." And he pulled away, leaving Josh in the silence of the crossroads.

Josh began to walk in the direction of the complex in the distance. With each minute, the place began to look more foreboding. From the shimmering heat, he could see the shapes of towers emerging from the corners of the low building.

What could possess him to send me here? Josh wondered. And then wondered yet again whether the crazy old man might just be crazy.

Maybe this is all *a myth*, he thought. *Perhaps none of it's true. I've been wandering around in some fairytale.*

Concrete. Fence. Gates. Buzzers. Cameras. Everywhere Josh looked he was reminded that, even though this was a minimum-security institution, it was still nothing like the outside world.

He stood waiting while yet another guard looked at his driver's license. He pressed a button, and the steel door in front of him buzzed. "Go ahead," the guard said, and Josh pulled the door open.

He walked down a short hall, then into an open cafeteria-like setting. A few inmates dressed in coveralls sat at tables speaking with family or friends, or perhaps lawyers—Josh couldn't tell. He scanned the room, unsure what to do next, and saw a handsomely rugged man sitting alone at a table. The man raised his arm in greeting, and Josh walked toward the table. As he got closer, Josh realized the man was probably older than he looked. He was clearly in excellent shape, but as Josh reached the table he could see the grey in his hair, and the wrinkles around his eyes.

"You must be Josh. I'm Travis." His voice was deep and gravelly, with a hint of southern drawl.

Josh shook the man's hand, and looked around the room again. He wasn't sure what to do.

"Welcome to Galliston, son. Don't worry—you'll get used to the place. I did long ago, unfortunately."

Josh opened his mouth, but nothing came out. Travis simply looked at him. "I'm not quite sure why I'm here," Josh finally said.

Travis looked at him, saying nothing, and it occurred to Josh that the man was in no rush. *Can you blame him?* He thought. But Cor had said he'd only get fifteen minutes.

Travis finally spoke. "The old man bring you?"

"He dropped me up the road. Didn't want to get the bike dirty. You know how he is about that bike."

Travis was quiet for a moment, as if deciding how to reply. "Oh, I know him quite well," he said at last. "I was once you, you know."

"You were?"

"Oh yeah. The trips on that damn bike. The meetings. I did all that." Travis looked around the bleak room and chuckled. "You might say I'm a cautionary tale of sorts."

Josh was taken aback. "I've had a pretty amazing week. Everyone I've met, everything I've seen and done . . . it's hard to imagine those things leading me anywhere close to . . . here. If your job is to scare me, I'm not sure it's necessary."

Travis eyed him silently. "That's exactly why it *is* my job," he said after a long pause. "Because you don't think it's necessary."

"I'm not sure I understand."

"Let's take a walk," Travis said.

Josh wondered where the hell they were going to walk to—weren't they in a *prison?* But he stood up and followed Travis as he strolled up to the guard. "We're going to take a walk, Mike," he said.

"Sure thing," Mike said. "Enjoy. Beautiful day out there."

Josh looked at the guard in surprise, but followed Travis as Mike unlocked first one door, then a second. The guard stepped aside to let them pass, and Josh found himself in a grassy area outside the prison. A chain link fence in the distance stood as a reminder that they weren't quite *outside* in the full sense of the word.

Travis began to walk toward the distant fence line. "What the old man is giving you," Travis began, "is some powerful stuff. As you might expect, I'm here to talk to you about another myth—about something you believe that you shouldn't. But I'm also here to impress upon you that power can work both ways.

It can do great things for you and others. Or it can cause great hardship."

"Is that what happened to you?"

Travis stopped at the fence line, and looked toward the distant trees. "I met Cor through a friend. Much like you, I imagine. At the time, I was struggling to build an investment firm, but clients—especially clients with money to invest—were hard to come by."

"I know that feeling," Josh said.

"Sure you do. And, correct me if I'm wrong, but I'm guessing you have some big material goals. Nice cars? A boat? Big house? Private jet, even?"

Josh smiled. "Guilty."

"Josh," Travis said, "I had—and still have—the most audacious financial goals. I wanted it *all*. Private islands, yachts, jets—the works.

"Like you, I spent a week with Cor. And to say my eyes were opened is an understatement. I felt like I'd discovered a whole new world. Everything I heard, everyone I met, seemed to speak to *me*. Eloise and her goal setting? That was me. I'd set these big financial goals all the time. But I never turned them into behaviors, so I never got anywhere."

Josh nodded. *Just like me*, he thought.

"And the Knowledge Myth? I was a poster boy for falling for that. Always looking for the magic bullet— the next big marketing thing or secret—until I met Anna, and I learned to do more of what I already knew.

"Hell, when I first heard the Failure Myth, I thought Nathan had written it just for me. I was paralyzed by the idea that I'd get something wrong and never reach my big goals, instead of realizing that failure might just bring me closer. And the Abundance Myth?"

Josh grinned, realizing what Travis would say.

"I'm not kidding. I was all about the getting, not the giving. I couldn't see past my own wallet to realize that abundance was about what I could give."

"And the Value Myth? They could have called that the Travis Myth, I fell for it so badly. I had been constantly trying to under-deliver so that my share was bigger. Melody taught me the truth about delivering the unexpected."

While Josh was sure Travis was exaggerating his own failures, the man's deprecating humor was somehow working. *Still*, Josh thought, *he's in prison!*

As if reading his mind, Travis spoke up. "It's okay, Josh. Everyone wants to know how I got here. You can ask."

"I admit I'm curious. Did you not understand what they were teaching?"

"I did better than understand what Cor and his friends were teaching, Josh. I *lived* it. It was like it climbed inside my DNA. I restructured my day, my business, my life. I lived those principles 24–7."

"Didn't they work?" Josh began to feel a knot forming in his stomach again. *What if this is all a waste?*

Travis let out another gravelly chuckle. "Stop *worrying*, son. Of *course* everything worked. I changed my life, my business, everything. I did everything I needed to, everything Cor's teachers told me to. I did it all. I set my behaviors. I started doing more instead of trying to know more. I began to take action without fear of failure. I started to *give*, and deliver huge amounts of unexpected value. The clients rolled in. People couldn't believe what I did for them. I literally did it all."

Josh shook his head. "But that doesn't make sense. You did everything right."

Travis stopped as they reached the door they'd started from.

"That's why you're here, Josh. You're right. I did *do* everything I was supposed to. I'm not here because of what I did. I'm here for a different reason."

Josh stared at him blankly. "Travis," he finally said, "I have no idea what the hell you're talking about."

Travis let out a deep, gravelly laugh. "I like you, son. Let's go see if we can get Mike to give us a few more minutes and I'll explain."

They entered the building again, and Mike returned them to the same room they started in. "Your time's up," he said. "But I guess we don't need to count the outside time, right?" Again, Josh found himself surprised by the guard's demeanor.

"Thanks, Mike," Travis said.

They walked back to their table, and took a seat.

"What did you mean," Josh began, "when you said you weren't here because of what you did?"

"You get a lot of time to think in here, Josh. It's part curse, part blessing. I've learned that *what* I did isn't the most important thing."

Josh felt a wave of confusion wash over him. "But don't actions determine our results? I feel like I've spent this whole week trying to take better action." Josh's voice began to rise and he was dimly aware that the guard was watching him. "The myths are all about doing. It's all *action*." He slumped back in his chair and laid his hands on the table in frustration. "And now you're telling me that it's not doing, it's something *else*. And that the doing can land me prison?"

Travis smiled. "I know it seems confusing. Don't be disheartened. Action is critical, but it's not *everything*."

He reached into his shirt pocket and pulled out several small pieces of paper and a pencil.

"You'll probably recognize this," he said. Travis took two slips of paper, and wrote one word on each:

_____   _DO_   _HAVE_

"That's what Eloise taught me on my first day with Cor," Josh said.

"And what does it mean?" Travis prodded gently.

"It means that in order to *have*—to reach our goals of material things, or accomplishments—we need to *do*. We have to work the goals back into behaviors. Into to-do's, literally. Most people get caught up in the future state of what they want—the goal—but neglect to turn it into present action." ✗

"Exactly," said Travis. "My job today is to add to that model."

Travis took a third slip of paper and added to the front of the sequence. Josh could see the sheet contained a single word: *Be*.

BE   DO   HAVE

Josh looked at the paper, then up at Travis. Then blinked. "I don't get it."

Travis smiled. "Neither did I. And that's why we're both here."

For the next few minutes, Travis told Josh the story of how his business had been transformed after he met Cor. "I look back now and I'm still amazed. It was a wonderful period in my life." Travis paused. "The problem was that it wasn't enough. I wanted more. More money. More stuff. And I wanted it a lot faster than it was coming."

"That doesn't sound so different from most people," Josh ventured.

"Maybe," Travis mused. "But the difference is that most people don't commit fraud to make it happen. One day

I did a small business favor for a friend. I bent the rules a little. He needed the help, and I did it out of friendship. But that was the first step on a slippery slope. I got away with it, made some quick money, started spending more money, doing more crooked deals to keep up the image and lifestyle. Within six months, I was doing far more crooked deals than straight ones. And then I moved on to the big money. Full-fledged scams. Ponzi schemes and huge financial cons. They were a lot easier, surprisingly. And even more lucrative." He paused, then smiled ruefully. "Until you get caught, of course. After that, it was like dominoes falling," he continued. "I was arrested. Released on bail, but the next six months were hell. I lost my assets, my business. And one day I came home—late as always—and my family was gone." Travis looked down at the blank scraps of paper in his hands. "My wife left. Took the kids. In hindsight, that was a smart move on her part, but at the time, I couldn't understand it. A few months later I was here. I had nothing. Nothing at all."

The last sentence hung in the air. Josh was the first to break the silence. He reached out and tapped the scrap of paper between them, pointing at the word *Be*. "How did this lead you here?"

"There's a natural flow to life, Josh. It can be hard to see at times, but it's there. Like the current in a very wide, slow river, it can be subtle. Most people, if they see it at all, see the flow like this." Travis rearranged the cards:

Have—Do—Be

Josh looked at the words then up at Travis.

"Most people want to *have* before they *do* and then finally *be*," Travis explained. "It's against the natural flow. It's like swimming upstream everyday fighting the current of life. And it's exactly what I was doing. I was swimming upstream. I was trying to *have* first and foremost. It didn't feel like I was swimming upstream at first. But I sure felt it when I landed here."

Josh moved the papers back into the Be-Do-Have sequence.

"Okay. So this is the correct sequence. I've certainly learned a lot about *doing*. But what do you mean by *Be*? I'm not sure I understand."

"*Be* refers to your state of being. I call it your *intention*."

Josh pursed his lips. "I don't know. I've heard that term before. It sounds like...mumbo-jumbo, or something."

"I had the same impression. But let me ask you this: Why is it that two people can *do* the same things, and yet get different results?"

Josh's mind flashed to Amy's sign on the Haltons' lawn. He and Amy offered the same service, same price. They probably gave the same presentation to prospects. "I don't know," he finally said. "But I can't argue the point. I see it happen all the time."

"I'll tell you why. The reason they get different results is because of their *intention*. It's not just what they *do*. It's who they *are* being when they're doing it."

Travis flipped over the *Be* piece of paper and slid it to Josh. It contained the Attraction Myth.

The Attraction Myth

Myth: We attract into our lives what we want to have.

Truth: We attract into our lives who we are.

Josh read the statement, trying to digest it.

"I'm not sure I understand completely. I want to apply this to my own situation, but how is who I am *being* stopping my business from growing? Do I need to be more personable?"

"*Being* is not your personality. It's your *intention*."

"Okay," Josh said, tentatively. "I'm not seeing this clearly. What *exactly* do you mean by intention?"

"Let me give you some examples of intentions, or states of being," Travis said. He took one more piece of paper and began to make a list in two columns.

Negative	Positive
Pessimistic	Optimistic
Selfish	Generous
Entitled	Grateful
Unhappy	Happy
Financially Irresponsible	Financially Responsible

Josh watched as he wrote the words. "I understand those states. But can you give me an example?"

"Sure. The typical way of thinking is that we need to *have* things in order to *do* things, and as a result we can *be* in a certain state. People believe, for example, they need to *have* more time, in order to *do* exercise, so they can *be* health conscious." With each word, Travis tapped his pencil on the Be-Do-Have card. "They think 'When I *earn* more money, then I'll *save* more, and I can *be* financially responsible."

"And that's backwards?"

"Of course. Working in the opposite direction changes everything. If you begin to *be* financially responsible, Josh—if that's your *intention*, then you start to behave differently. You make your bill payments on time. You save. You invest. And that changes what you *have* financially."

Josh thought of his missed mortgage payment. It seemed as if it happened a hundred years ago, but he felt his cheeks flush.

"The same goes for your business. My intention was negative. It was to *get* as much as I could from every interaction. You've been introduced to people this week who have the *completely opposite* intention. Every one of them is wildly successful."

Josh thought about Amy. *Her intention is to help—to give—and mine has always been to get, get a listing, get a sale.* A faint tickle of insight began to appear in Josh's stomach, but before he could question Travis, the guard approached their table. *Damn!* Josh thought. *We're out of time!*

Instead of telling them their time was up, though, Mike placed two ice-cold sodas on the table in front of them. "Funny thing happened," he said in a low voice. "Someone forgot to write down the time your guest arrived, Travis. How about we reset the clock for another five." He looked at Josh, winked, and walked away. To Josh's amazement, he then walked across the room and abruptly *ended* the visit of a man and woman at a distant table. Josh looked back at Travis, astonished by the guard's paradoxical behavior. Travis just smiled and shrugged. "Be, do, have, Josh," he said. "It even works in jail."

"How do you get this special treatment?"

"I've chosen to control my intention here. To be grateful for what I've learned, rather than resentful. To give to the guards, instead of seeing them as taking my freedom from me. They respond to that intention."

Travis looked at the clock. "Let's finish up, Josh. Just remember: What you're learning applies to everyone, everywhere. To every*thing*. It's more than just a new truth," Travis continued. "It's a filter to see *all* the new truths through. For example, you can choose to see abundance as just the action of *giving*, but it becomes so much more powerful when you see *yourself* as someone who *gives*. *Being* generous is a far more powerful state than a *quid-pro-quo* equation." Travis swept the pieces of paper from the table, and held them out to Josh, who pocketed them. Travis stood and walked Josh toward the door at the guard station.

"The one thing you can control in life, Josh, is your state of being. Your *intention*. The things you *have?* They can be taken from you in an instant. Trust me on that one. Your job. Your home. Your loved ones. Your possessions. You can never fully control what happens to the outside of your life. But the inside? Who you are being? Your *intention?* That's something that's entirely yours to own. Always."

As they reached the door, Josh paused. "I'm surprised Cor didn't come with me to visit you. You must not get many visitors."

"You know him and that damn bike," Travis drawled. Then he became somber. "I told you how I met Cor," he said. "But I never told you how we parted."

"Parted?"

"I was Cor's protégé, you might say. His biggest success story. We were like father and son."

"What happened?" Josh asked.

"Isn't it obvious? I scammed him, Josh. I took his money. Lots of it. He was my last big con."

Josh was stunned.

"Is that why he didn't drive me all the way here?"

Travis looked at him. "Quite the opposite. He chose to forgive me. In fact, he paid for my legal defense. If it weren't for him, my sentence would be twice as long." He paused, then reached out and shook Josh's hand.

"The old man lives this stuff, son," he said. "You'd be wise to do the same."

And with that Travis turned away and Mike closed the heavy steel door.

The Attraction Myth

Myth: We attract into our lives what we want to have.

Truth: We attract into our lives who we are being. ✓

Chapter 10

The Journal

Four hours later, Josh tipped his head back onto the headrest of the car, his heart pounding. *So close*, he thought.

It was over.

The prospect had been as big a deal as Josh had suspected. But in the end, if anything, he was *too* big.

What he wanted was something that no one in this area could provide. It simply couldn't be done. He'd told the man that, thanked him for his time, and now it was time to face reality: *It was over*. He'd landed a big fish, but he didn't have a boat big enough to get him to shore.

There was no way he'd make it into the top ranks now. That meant his job was gone, and if that were the case, then he couldn't see how paying the mortgage and car payments was going to happen, never mind the regular bills and day-to-day living expenses.

The negative voice was back. *And?* it asked.

If he was really honest with himself, he wasn't confident about what would happen with Kiera. He sighed. His whole body felt so heavy. He just wanted to go to sleep. He closed his eyes.

We get who we are being. It was as if Travis's deep southern drawl was right in his ear.

Josh opened his eyes. "I just fell for the Attraction Myth," he said aloud. "I just told myself that I couldn't close a big deal. That I couldn't pay my bills. That I couldn't even make my *marriage* work."

I'll be damned, he thought. *What did Travis tell me to do? Change my focus or change my behavior.*

"There must be some way to figure this out," he said aloud, with far more enthusiasm than he felt. He looked in the mirror.

Were you expecting something to happen? the voice said.

"I guess not," he sighed.

He was about to slip the car into drive when he caught something from the corner of his eye. It was the success journal from the sales seminar he'd been to the previous week. He vaguely remembered it being on the passenger seat on his drive back from the workshop. *It slid to the floor when you hit the brakes at the Haltons' house that night*, he recalled.

He picked it up from the floor, and was about to toss it on the passenger seat when he stopped. *Change your behaviors*, he thought, and opened it instead.

Inside the book was the list of goals Josh had carefully crafted over the course of the workshop. Some were lofty, others more tangible, but just in reading them he felt some of the enthusiasm flow back into him that he'd felt when he'd made them. Jotted all through the margins were tiny notes, most with exclamation points, stars, or smiley faces. Josh began to flip through the pages, surprised at how many ideas there were.

Wow, Josh thought. *I was really on fire that weekend*.

As he scanned the margins, one scrawled phrase caught his attention. It was darkly circled, as if he'd gone over and over it with his pen for emphasis. Josh had no recollection of writing it, but as he read the phrase, he remembered it had been just one more idea of many, triggered at the time by something happening in the room. What the trigger was, he had no idea, but as he read the words, he could feel his mind begin to shift into gear.

Josh went over the events of that weekend. He could almost feel it again, that energy of being in a room of like-minded people; the clarity of letting go of the day-to-day chaos, and opening up to possibilities.

Maybe it wasn't a waste after all, he thought.

Josh looked at the idea again, turned it over in his mind. And then Wendy's words came back to him:

It's like we never even talk, never mind actually work together.

That's what she'd said. She'd been describing how lonely their profession was. Josh looked back again at his journal. *Why couldn't it work?*

Josh hesitated a moment more, then grabbed his phone. A now-familiar voice answered. "Wendy," he said. "It's Josh. Where are you?"

"At the office. Where you should be. We just had our weekly roundtable. Every agent is in. Now's not a good time to be missing meetings, Josh."

"Forget about it. Can you get them all to stay?"

"Stay?"

"Yes. All of them. I'll explain when I get there. Just ask them for 15 minutes of their time. I'll be there in ten." There was silence on the phone. *Come on, Wendy*, Josh pleaded silently.

"You got it, Josh. I'll put on more coffee and lock the doors if I have to."

Josh exhaled.

"I'll see you in ten minutes."

■　■　■

Josh pulled up in front of the building, shut off the engine, and then took a deep breath.

This had better fly.

He had 15 minutes with two dozen very busy people. He didn't want to screw it up. He had no desire to fail in front of all his colleagues.

Fail? a new voice said.

"Okay," he said aloud. "I have no desire to make this a poignant learning moment on the road to success. That better?" Then he laughed, and felt the tension drain out of him.

Let's go, Josh. You can do this.

"I pretty much have to at this point," he said to the empty car.

Then he stepped out, and headed for the door.

■ ■ ■

Josh left the meeting feeling cautiously optimistic. He'd at least convinced them to *try*. And that was something. But he'd have to make the damn thing *work*. And that meant he had just a few hours to hit three more brokerages, including Amy's, and convince them all to try. He took a deep breath. "Let's get going, then," he said aloud, and put the car in gear.

Chapter 11

The Shop

Josh pulled into Cor's laneway for what he knew would be the last time.

It's over, he thought. *A good try. But it's over.*

He had no ill-feelings toward Cor or Amy. He'd enjoyed the week, he learned a lot, and didn't begrudge the time he'd spent with them. *If anything*, Josh thought, *I feel guilty that I wasted their time*. That thought followed him down the laneway, and he took a deep breath as he saw Amy's car parked in front of the shop. Time to face the music.

■ ■ ■

"Ironically, I got the seeds of the idea at that sales seminar," said Josh. He smiled weakly at Amy. "I know," Josh said. "You told me not to feel bad about learning. You were right."

"That's the thing about those types of investments, Josh," Amy said. "You're investing on the inside. And so change happens on the inside, too. And that can take a while to show up on the outside."

In my case, I guess it didn't show up at all, Josh thought. Then he banished the voice. He was determined to finish this on a positive note.

"Let's hear the idea," Cor said.

"It doesn't matter much now," Josh said.

"Then I guess you've got time to tell us," Cor said.

Josh sighed. "Of all the myths, the one that resonated with me the most was the Value Myth. It seemed so relevant to my industry. People like Amy and I... we're struggling to add enough *value*. People don't really need an agent to shuffle paperwork around or show someone a house. Those are important things, sure, but," he looked over at Cor's gleaming motorcycles. "They're just polish. Not true value."

Cor smiled.

"I'd been racking my brains trying to come up with something new. As I discovered, it's hard to just come up with a great idea on the spot. Sometimes you need inspiration. And I guess I must have been inspired during that sales weekend, because the answer was right in my journal."

"That's a big part of the value of those things," Amy said. "Inspiration comes from many places, but not always from within. The speakers, the participants, the panels, the stories. Anytime you put people in a room like that, there's huge potential."

Josh nodded. "Ever since I started in this industry, it's been drilled into me that listings are key. You need sellers to list their homes for sale, and then you need to sell them to buyers. Pretty simple. But I believe that for every home that's listed, there are probably another ten that are *almost* for sale. They're homes that could be sold if the right buyer came along, but the owners aren't actively seeking to sell. They aren't interested in getting involved in *potentially* selling their home— listing the place, having hoards of people through. That's just too much trouble. They're just not ready to put their home on the open market.

"Some agents try to target those homes. They knock on doors occasionally with a buyer in mind. But the problem is that you can't know every home. Especially the unique, pricier ones. But," Josh said. "A hundred real estate agents *can*."

"Today," Josh continued, "I saw this crowd of agents and they nearly made me late for my appointment. I was frustrated as hell, but a part of me kept thinking about the *power* of that crowd. After all, if a bunch of people can stop a moving car . . . what could a whole crowd of real estate agents accomplish?"

He looked at Amy. "Think about it," he said. "Between you and me and every other agent, we probably know every property in the area. I realized we just needed a way to *pool* our knowledge. Not about homes already for sale, but about those that *aren't but might be.*"

Amy was sitting upright now, paying close attention.

"Well I figured there were two parts. The first was getting more specific information about what our buyers want, getting into details of the perfect home, property, neighborhood. Really finding out what drives them.

"And then," he said. "Instead of only trying to sell them something that's *already* for sale, which they can find themselves easily with today's technology, we tap into the pool of agent knowledge to find a few *ideal* homes by sharing what our clients *really* want. The clients are happier, the agents do more deals, and everyone wins."

Amy was excited. "It's something we can't do now because we don't really *know* what other people's clients want. In fact," she added, "most of the time we don't even know what our own clients want. We're just trying to sell them what we have instead of what they need."

"Exactly. We're trying to hammer square pegs into round holes. There's no abundance there. No value. So I made up a simple system for really capturing what our buyers want. It's just paper right now, but we can easily share it online with some simple computer work. And if every agent used it, we could all more readily find properties that fit."

"Josh," cried Amy. "I love it. What an idea."

"It's a sort of crowd-sourcing," Josh said. "As a whole, we know more than we do individually. Together, all of us are smarter than any one of us. It's a bit like potluck math. We end up with more in the end." Then his face fell.

Josh sighed. "I guess it doesn't matter much at this stage. I mean . . . it's still a good idea, I think. But it didn't work. I tried it with nearly 100 agents yesterday. No one had any ideas for my client." He held up his hand in a "stop" motion without even looking up from the floor.

"Before you say it, I know. It's just a waypoint on the path to success. But it was a pretty crucial one. I missed the top spots on our team so this particular failure is going to be a fork in the path. I'm going to have to find a new route to success." He sighed. "Kiera's going to kill me."

Amy looked puzzled. "You tried it yesterday? How come I never heard anything?"

Josh shrugged. "You weren't at your office when I pitched the idea. I figured you didn't want to make me nervous," he smiled. "Anyway. My client had this specific need. He wanted a huge acreage of rural property to build his dream home. But he wanted an income from the acreage. Have you ever tried to find a thousand acres of land around here? All these little vineyards. It's an impossible task. There aren't more than 100 acres for sale at any one time." Josh looked wistfully out the shop door at the rolling hills.

"It would have been a hell of a deal, though, I'll tell you that." Josh became aware that the room had gone silent. He looked up to see Amy standing there with her mouth agape. "What?"

"Josh," Amy laughed, snapping out of her shock. "I know the perfect property."

The room was silent for a moment, but for Josh, that moment felt like a long, swirling, slow-motion eternity. It was as if he was watching from afar as disparate pieces of his life spun and danced and finally clicked together in a huge patchwork. The success weekend. Amy. Cor. The myths. Even that damn motorcycle. They all clicked into place and created one perfect moment where everything came together.

Cor had gone back to his motorcycles, seemingly unsurprised, although Josh noted a small smile playing around the corner of his mouth. Josh opened his mouth but nothing came out. "You—you know a property," he finally croaked.

"It's not listed . . . but I know the owner. He wants to sell."

"You're kidding me."

"No. I'm serious."

"Can . . . can . . ." Josh was stuttering. "Where is he?!" he blurted out.

Amy stood there, shaking her head in wonder. "He's right here."

She looked over to where Cor sat at the workbench with the same smile playing around his mouth. He was shaking his head ever so slightly, pleased, but not surprised the way Josh clearly was.

Josh's mouth still hung open. *Could this really be true?*

Chapter 12

The Happiness Myth

Josh woke up the next morning to an unfamiliar feeling: *peace*. He looked over to where Kiera lay sleeping. *What a day*, he thought.

After Amy's revelation the day before, the afternoon had passed in a blur. Never had Josh known a deal to go through so quickly, but in hindsight, why wouldn't it? He'd found the only property within a few hundred miles that met the buyer's needs. The rest was just paperwork.

Josh slipped out of bed and padded to the kitchen in his pajamas. As he made coffee, he thought about the strange road that had led him to this moment. Standing here in his kitchen, on a perfect day, with everything feeling right with the world.

He looked out the window, and watched a woman push a stroller down the street. His mind flashed back to earlier in the week.

Almost perfect, he thought, his mood shifting. *But close enough . . . right?*

Josh poured his coffee, then paused and took an extra cup from the cupboard for Kiera. He'd surprise her with coffee in bed, and then he was looking forward to reading the paper and relaxing for a few hours.

But something had changed. Josh sat in the sunshine, trying to conjure up the feeling of perfection he'd felt when he'd first awoken, but it had slipped away. *It's no use*, he thought.

He sat for another half hour, staring out the window, not able to believe that he was truly thinking about doing what he was about to do.

Finally, he reached for the phone.

Two hours later, Josh stood in Carl's office, in the place where this had all started a week earlier.

Carl was dressed in old jeans and a sweatshirt. Josh had pulled him away from a morning of yard work. Now he leaned back in his chair and silently appraised Josh for what seemed like the hundredth time that morning. "Are you sure about this?"

Josh paused, for just a brief moment. "Yeah. I'm sure."

"Okay," Carl sighed. "Then it's done."

Josh felt a sudden sense of panic, then, just as quickly, a calm surety like he'd never experienced. He smiled.

"Thanks, Carl. I'll clear out my desk this week."

Carl stared at him yet again, deep in thought.

"Actually, you'll do it tomorrow morning," he finally said. "First thing."

Josh was a bit taken aback and fought back his irritation. "That's fine. I'll be here."

"And," Carl continued, "You'll move to the empty office next door to me. You're going to need the space."

It was Josh's turn to stare. "I don't understand."

■ ■ ■

Josh drove the quiet Sunday morning streets toward home. A sense of wonder still flowed through him. Everything seemed different: The people walking, the morning sounds of grass being cut, and even something he'd never noticed before: the sounds of Sunday church bells. It seemed to all fit together in sort of chaotic, yet perfect symphony.

What a week it had been. He felt so completely different than he had just days earlier. Even when he had left the sales seminar, high on adrenaline and potential, he hadn't felt like *this*.

Josh realized that, in that moment, what he was feeling was *happiness*. He was, for perhaps the first time, truly *happy*. What a week, indeed. The church bells sounded again, fading now in the distance as he drove.

Church bells.

Josh's mind began to churn, his mental wheels turning against something he couldn't quite see.

What a week.

And then it clicked. He turned the car around.

It was Sunday, but Josh wasn't surprised to find Cor in his shop, tinkering. Then he realized: Cor was *packing*. Of course. Cor spotted Josh, and waved him over. "I know I have some time, but I figured I might as well get started," Cor explained.

"How can I help?" Josh said.

"You can start putting those boxes together," said Cor. "But you can also tell me what brings you here. After yesterday, it seems to me like you don't need any more help."

Josh grinned. "It was quite a day. And...thank you. For everything."

Cor shrugged. "You're welcome, Josh. Just remember to pass it on, like Amy did."

"Oh, don't worry. I will. But first," Josh set down the box he was assembling, "I have a bone to pick with you."

Cor didn't look up, but Josh could tell the old man's small smile was dancing around the corners of his mouth again. "Really?" Cor said.

"Yeah. Really. I realized it on the way home this morning. Today is Sunday."

"And?" Cor said, but Josh could tell he was feigning confusion.

"And that means it's day seven. You told me there were seven myths. I've only learned six of them. So, who do we meet today?"

Cor laughed.

"You're right. But I can tell you two things. First is that you've already learned all seven. Secondly, you've already met the person who taught you the last myth."

"I don't understand. I met one person each day for six days."

"I didn't say you had to meet a new person, Josh. The last person is someone you know quite well."

"Who?" Josh asked, confused. Then it hit him: *Amy.*

"Let's go find out, shall we?" Cor said, smiling mischievously.

"Another ride on the Cub?" Josh asked. "That's one thing I won't miss."

"No, Josh. I think this time we'll walk."

A short while later, Josh and Cor were walking past the rows of grapevines on one of the adjacent fields to Cor's shop, which, Josh now knew, also belonged to Cor. As did the next one, and so on.

Cor's assembled property totaled just over one thousand acres, a vast amount, both in physical space and in *value.*

"I want to thank you again for making the deal come together for me," Josh said.

"It was you that made it come together," Cor replied. "You created the value."

He was right, Josh supposed. He had done it, but not without help. Not without the myths.

For the next 15 minutes, Josh told Cor the latest news. He recounted the story of that morning. How he'd given a small share of the enormous deal—a career-maker, to be sure—to Wendy to help her through a tight spot.

It had felt right, somehow, he explained to Cor. "It was talking to her that really made the idea gel," he said. "If she hadn't talked about how lonely this job is, none of this would have happened. It was just the right thing to do."

There was more good news. Carl had offered to create a new job for Josh. His idea for adding value had struck a chord. His new job would be to harness the collective brains of every agent in the region, and create the systems and support so that what had happened with Cor and Amy yesterday could be replicated by agents everywhere. He'd get a huge raise, a challenging new job, and a great bonus structure, too. Everything had worked out perfectly.

In addition, Josh would be the new internal company trainer. He'd help other sales professionals become more productive. That, in turn, would mean Carl wouldn't have to downsize.

"He's taking a risk," Josh said. "But it means that, for now, we all keep our jobs. And the first person I coach will be Wendy."

"And can I ask what you plan to teach these people?" Cor said. Josh didn't have to look to know the old man was smiling.

"I've got something in mind," Josh grinned. "A seven-step process, to be precise."

Josh stopped walking. "Of course, I could use some input on the seventh one. I'm a little vague there." He looked across the vast tapestry of land before him. And then it hit him. He turned to Cor, grinning.

"It's not Amy who we're meeting, is it. It's me. Right? The last person I had to meet. I'm the person."

"I knew the moment I met you that you were a bright man, Josh. Yes. The last myth you needed to learn could only be learned by meeting yourself—the *true* you."

"The true me?"

"I believe there is only one state when we are our true selves, Josh. And it's the state you reached today. It's one that everyone strives for, but few reach. The state of being your authentic self."

Josh looked at him, uncertain.

"Remember what Travis told you about how important your state is? That's what this is all about. Changing what's on the inside. Each one of the myths you discovered was about changing your *mind*. They're all about the *Be* part of the equation.

"I believe we all have one state in which we are our best selves. It's the most powerful state of all. One in which we make almost perfect decisions, take perfect action, and get perfect results."

"That sounds pretty good to me," Josh laughed.

"It is," Cor acknowledged. "And it's why we need to work so hard to unlearn the Success Myths. They stand in the way of finding that perfect state. Not the state of wealth, or material abundance, but the state you found today. That's what we all long for."

Josh looked at Cor, puzzled.

"It's the state of being *happy*, Josh. Isn't that what you are today? Right now?"

Josh smiled. "I am. Truly, I think. But I don't understand how that's a myth."

"Being happy isn't a myth, Josh. But having happiness is."

"Now you've completely lost me. Isn't that just... semantics? Wordplay?"

"Perhaps, but it illustrates the point. Everyone's striving for happiness, Josh. They want happiness like it's a *thing*. It's what happened to Travis. He wanted happiness like something you can buy, or have. But it's not. It's something you choose in any moment. You choose your state of being.

"You found happiness by sharing one of the greatest sales deals in recent memory around here. But you didn't find happiness, the *thing*. You *became* happy."

Josh knew Cor was right. "I *am* happy. But what is the happiness myth?"

"That you can't *have* happiness, Josh. You can only *be* it. Just like you are right now."

■ ■ ■

As Josh and Cor reached the front of the shop door, Josh turned to him.

"There's something that's been bothering me," he said. "About the Success Myths."

Cor looked at him. Josh could see he'd caught the older man off guard.

"It seems to me that," Josh said, "the myths themselves . . ." he struggled for the right words, " . . . they
aren't entirely wrong."

"What do you mean?" Cor asked.

"Well. Failure really *can* be bad. It can hurt. It can
cause terrible harm and great loss. And goals—they're
not bad things in themselves. And there *is* value in
just giving people a baker's dozen. Lots of successful
businesses work on that principle. It seems to me,"
Josh repeated, "That the myths aren't *myths*."

Cor laughed. "Josh, you are absolutely right. The
reality is that every myth has a kernel of truth at its
core. You're a wise man if you can find that kernel,
and hang onto it, and throw away the things that don't
resonate." He looked around at the rusted carcasses
of long-dead machines in the tall grass. "Henry Ford
once said that if he'd asked people what they wanted,
they'd have said a faster horse. You need to decide
what it is that *you* believe, Josh. It's part of finding
your authentic self." He started to walk into the shop,
then turned back to Josh. "They may be *my myths*,
Josh. But your job is to make them *your truths*. Only
you can do that."

As he stood in the big doorway, watching Cor dis-
appear inside, Josh saw a taxi coming down the

laneway. It stopped near the open bay door, and Josh was surprised to see Amy step out.

"Are you okay?" Josh asked. "Where's your car?"

Amy's eyes twinkled. "I'm fine, Josh."

"Why did you take a cab?"

"Josh." Cor had emerged from the shop, wiping his hands with a rag. "Amy's taking your car home for you."

Josh was confused. "What . . . where am I going?"

"I have something for you."

Josh followed him into the shop, and Cor led him to the back.

He grabbed an old, grease-stained drop cloth and gave it a yank. Underneath, was the gleaming Honda Cub. Josh looked at Cor.

"It's for you, Josh."

"I—I—can't. This is," he trailed off. "I can't."

"I'm getting too old for the damn thing anyway," Cor said. "It's a wonder I didn't kill both of us."

"Well. You did severely injure my pride on several occasions."

Josh looked at the old man, and saw tears welling in his eyes even as he smiled. He handed Josh the leather helmet and goggles he'd worn so many times. "Be happy, Josh," he said.

Josh embraced Cor and Amy, and said his goodbyes. As he started the bike and it purred steadily, he noticed the license plate: BE JOSH. He looked at Cor with a smile. "Just be, Josh," the old man said. "It's enough."

Minutes later, Josh was speeding down the road on the Honda Cub, his face open and smiling in the autumn sun.

The Happiness Myth

> **Myth:** You can have happiness.
> **Truth:** You can't have happiness.
> You can only be it.

■ ■ ■

THE END